CULTURAL ANTHROPOLOGY

A CUSTOM READER
FOR CITRUS COLLEGE

Custom Publishing

New York   Boston   San Francisco
London   Toronto   Sydney   Tokyo   Singapore   Madrid
Mexico City   Munich   Paris   Cape Town   Hong Kong   Montreal

**Pearson
Custom Publishing**
is a division of

www.pearsonhighered.com   ISBN 10: 0-536-45373-X

Contents

1

Career Advice for Anthropology Undergraduates

John T. Omohundro

In the previous article we learned that anthropologists regularly use their skills in the world of work and that employers are beginning to recognize the value of employees who are trained in anthropology. But the fact remains that many Americans do not fully understand what anthropology is and have little idea what students who major in anthropology can do for them. Worse, students themselves may not consciously recognize the work skills that anthropology has taught them or how to translate these skills into a language prospective employers can understand. John Omohundro tackles this problem of recognition and translation in this selection. Using a concept he calls "transcultural presentation," he lists some of the skills that anthropology teaches students and shows how these skills can be translated by graduating students into résumé language for employers.

The following scene happens at least once a semester. A distraught student pokes her (or his) head through my office door.

"Scuse me. . . . Are you busy? I need to ask you something."

"No, Grebbleberry, come in, sit down. What's bothering you?"

"Well, I really like anthropology. In fact, I want to drop my major in [deleted] and declare anthropology. But I told my parents and they were freaked out. My mother cried and my father threatened to cut me off. And my friends think I've lost it completely. Now they have me scared. I'm afraid I won't be able to get a job. What am I going to do?"

This student has all the symptoms of anthro shock. I'm tempted to smile in recognition of the syndrome but to Grebbleberry there is nothing amusing here. I have two answers: the difficult answer and the easy answer. The difficult answer, which I would like to give, is a problem because students are not prepared to believe me. The difficult answer is:

"For most careers, it doesn't matter much what you major in, as long as you like the subject and are good at it. The point of a major in a liberal arts education is to give practice at studying something in depth. One's major is not the same thing as job training. The careers that follow from most undergraduate majors are not and cannot be specified, even if the world doesn't change—but it does, frequently. There is no direct, obvious, and inevitable connection between college disciplines and the occupational titles people carry."

Although many years of teaching and advising convince me that the difficult answer I've just described is true, I don't respond with that answer anymore. First, I have to treat the "anthro shock"—the fear gripping the student that, ". . . mocked and alone, I'm going to starve." So, instead I reply with the easy answer:

"Take courage. There are many things you can do for a living that use your anthropological knowledge and skills. I can help you discover them and prepare for them."

Only then does the student's color begin to return; the anthro shock is in remission. Later, perhaps, after we've begun a career development program, I might introduce the difficult answer. But Grebbleberry still won't believe me, because my answer goes against most of what pundits, peers, parents, and even some professors have told her. This article presents some of the evidence that I have gathered for the claims made in the "easy" answer, to assist advisors to respond quickly and effectively to anthro shock.

Becoming a Career Advisor

Good advice is sorely needed and in short supply. Too many of the students I have supervised appeared flustered and ill-prepared when people ask them naive but usually sincere questions about what anthropology is, what it is good for, and what the student is going to "do with it." My advisees usually answered these questions apologetically or parried them with self-deprecating humor. Bill

Gates can get away with being apologetic and self-deprecating; my students need to present themselves more positively. Furthermore, many students and parents acquire their understanding of anthropology through students rather than professors, so it behooves us to raise the quality of the understanding that our major students impart. In turn, by improving their self-presentation our students will become more confident, more ambitious, and ultimately more successful in finding good work.

My career advising grew out of efforts to be a good teacher of the liberal arts, one who helps students move on to self-actualization in the world after college. The advising also grew out of my research in adaptive problem-solving by residents of small coastal communities in Newfoundland. Using the adaptive problem-solving approach, I ask, how do students find out about the world of work and how do they find their place in it? Twenty years ago, I began to develop career workshops within my department, then expanded them into workshops at anthropology conferences, and lately assembled those materials into a workbook, *Careers in Anthropology* (1998).[1] I use the book as a supplementary text in courses, as a workbook in careers workshops, and as an advising guide to students who declare anthropology as a major. This article is drawn from that book.

Because my experience with careers has been limited to academic ones, I collaborate with my college's career planning counselor. Lacking important parts of the whole picture, we are insufficient individually to advise anthropology majors. I have learned about résumés, interviews, and employer expectations, while my career planning colleagues have learned about the usefulness of anthropological perspectives and methods. Even if students consult both of us separately, they tend to perceive us as talking past one another, so they sometimes become frustrated and drop out of the process. But when the career planner and I work together, we see the value in each other's knowledge and how to blend it with concepts from our own fields. The career planners, for example, are delighted to learn that anthropology includes training in participant observation, object reconstruction and cataloging, and cognitive mapping, among other activities. They in turn have taught me what employers call those activities and how to highlight them on student résumés to increase what linguistic anthropologists call "indexicality," or talking on the same wavelength.

While working with the career planners, and counseling and tracking my advisees, I discovered that undergraduate anthropology alumni not only find meaningful work in which they use their anthropology, but they can use their anthropology to get hired to do that work. To demonstrate this idea I drafted and field tested exercises in which anthropological research techniques, such as ethnosemantics, life history, demography, participant observation, social network analysis, key informant interviews, and survey data analysis, are applied

---

[1]John T. Omohundro, *Careers in Anthropology* (Mountain View, CA: Mayfield Publishing Company, 1998).

to the tasks of selecting and pursuing interesting work. I also realized that when they are advising for careers, professors can use anthropological perspectives and data-collection techniques to better understand what students and employers know and need. Let us look briefly at what that might be.

Career Planning in Cross-Cultural Perspective

Except for a handful of publications distributed by the American Anthropological Association, few anthropologists have addressed the subject of career planning for undergraduate majors. One exception, James Spradley's "Career Education from a Cultural Perspective,"[2] shaped my conception of the problem. Spradley observes that in most cultures, such as the Amish in northern New York, the Inuit in central Canada, or the Masai in Kenya, children live close to the world of adult work. As they approach their own adulthood, youths understand clearly what adult work is and what they must do to take it up. There aren't many choices, but there isn't much anxiety either. The transition is smooth and supported by ritual, such as coming-of-age ceremonies.

The modern West, Spradley continues, is quite different. Career options are unclear to the beginner. A gulf yawns between their lives and what adults do. What kinds of careers are there over that gulf? What do people do in those positions? How do I decide which position is for me? How do I cross this gulf and get into the picture? The small-scale, nonindustrial cultures allowed twenty years of enculturation to adult careers. By comparison, Spradley observes, the postindustrial world expects youths to make a more complex transition from sixteen years of schooling to adult work in a matter of months or as little as a single weekend. And our culture has no ritual to ease the change.

It takes each student a while to assemble some kind of bridge across that gulf between college life and adult life. The average length of time in the U.S. between graduating with a B.A. and getting hired is six months to one year. That delay isn't usually because there aren't any jobs for liberal arts students. The delay is largely a cultural problem: new graduates simply don't know what to do next. A career counselor at Dartmouth College puts the problem like this: "Although liberal arts majors are qualified for dozens of jobs, they have no idea how to market themselves successfully."[3] They eventually figure it out and get back in the picture. Two years after graduation, two-thirds are employed full time (many of the others are in further study). Three-quarters of the employed are in positions related to their field of study.

---

[2]James P. Spradley, "Career Education from a Cultural Perspective," in Larry McClure and Carolyn Buan (eds.), *Essays in Career Education* (Portland, OR: Northwest Regional Educational Laboratory, 1973), pp. 3–16.

[3]Burton Nadler, *Liberal Arts Power: What It Is and How to Sell It on Your Resume,* 2nd ed. (Princeton, NJ: Peterson's, 1989).

My counseling efforts have aimed to enculturate students to the career life while they are still in college, thus abbreviating that liminal state after the baccalaureate degree. Of course, that's a tactical calculation. Looking back on sixteen years of formal education and looking ahead to a worklife of forty or more years, many of my advisees want to enter a liminal state for awhile. Nevertheless, other students are eager to move on. Those who made the effort during their college years to select a starting career, identify some employers, and prepare themselves for that career were rewarded by finding interesting work more quickly than those who waited until after they graduated. Students will have to make some time for this work in a busy college life. As my career planning colleague says, "Looking for a job is itself a job."

If students take up this job of career planning, their anthropology teachers can be valuable motivators and informants. However, not all professors say much about careers to their advisees or their classes. I know this is so because for years I have advised students from other colleges who sought me out at conferences, or when they were home visiting their parents, because they were suffering from anthro shock untreated by their own professors.

Why are some professors avoiding giving career advice? Some feel that after years in the ivory tower they don't understand the work world that their students want to enter. Times have changed, they say, since they were looking for a position. It is widely repeated in the college community that after graduation many students will enter careers that don't exist yet. Also, it is widely repeated that most people change careers (not just employers, but lines of work) several times in their working life. My career planning colleagues have amassed evidence to support these popular conceptions. So, "how can we know what to advise students today?" some of my colleagues wonder. Other professors define career advice, just as they do elementary writing instruction, as a task someone else should do.

A third reason that some professors avoid counseling for careers is that they don't approve of the idea of college as a place to credential people for jobs. In their view, student "vocationalism," or seeing college as a route to a good career, shifts the professor's role from liberator of young minds to gatekeeper of yuppiedom. Professors who teach critical approaches to culture want to inculcate resistance and a desire to change, not a desire to join, the system.

Anthropologist Michael Moffatt, in an insightful ethnography of residence halls and student culture, caused me to re-think student concern about jobs.[4] Moffatt suggests that professors who disdain student "vocationalism" are being hypocritical. After all, professors got their job by going to college, so why shouldn't the students want the same? Students expect that what they call their "job" will place them in the American middle classes, where their occupation will be a key element in their identity. They expect that job to offer them challenge, growth, rewards, security, and a chance to make the world a better place—all of which are goals deserving support from anthropology professors.

---

[4]Michael Moffat, *Coming of Age in New Jersey* (Brunswick, NJ: Rutgers University Press, 1986).

Translating the Skills

What does the student need to find that job and thus meet those goals? Career advice is partly a matter of teaching students to imagine themselves in a new way (the ethnographic "other's" way) and to construct a few basic models of what it's like in the working world.

Imagining themselves in a new way involves learning what employers (one of those ethnographic "others") really want (or think they want) and then reviewing one's education and experience for evidence of having acquired those desirable qualities. Seen in an anthropological light, this process may be called "trans-cultural self-presentation" and is similar to what the ethnographer initiates when entering the field and attempting to build rapport. Here are some data to assist that process.

Anthro shock contains the fear that one will acquire no marketable skills. "Marketable skills" implies there are other kinds as well. In fact, there are few skills that a liberal arts student acquires that aren't marketable. But there are temporary enthusiasms influencing which skills are considered desirable this year and what vocabulary is used to describe those skills. Anthropology students are well equipped to examine language, identify trends, and adapt to them by translating their own skills and knowledge into language appropriate for the setting.

Table 1 describes some skills that anthropology majors have an opportunity to develop at my college and, I am sure, at many other undergraduate institutions supporting a major. These are phrased in language immediately recognizable by the anthropology student and teacher.

Table 2 identifies twelve abilities often acquired through the undergraduate anthropology major. Fewer students and teachers will recognize their major as rephrased in this table, but employers will take notice. I advise my students to select anthropology and other courses intentionally to increase their competence in the abilities listed in Table 1 and then, when presenting themselves to potential graduate schools or employers, to highlight those abilities in the terms used in Table 2. Summer jobs, internships, volunteer work, as well as college classes may provide practice in the desirable activities (read "marketable skills").

Advanced majors in our senior seminar practice this transcultural self-presentation with exercises in composing résumé language. I begin by examining a résumé as a cultural text, an element in the process of seeking and offering jobs. We consider when and how their intended readers approach résumés. I argue that the résumé, in little more than a page, is intended to provoke interest in the writer as a person who can do (or learn to do) what the reader wants. In one column students list in their own language the experiences, both in their major and in their lives, that they think might have value. In a second column they conduct the "first-order" extraction of what skills and abilities were expected or practiced in those activities. In the third column they rephrase these skills and abilities in résumé language. Usually an anxiety-generating activity, composing résumés this way seems to generate more self-confidence.

TABLE 1   Some Transferable Skills in the
Anthropology Major

—Interacting with people of diverse cultures, making allowance for difference in
   customs and beliefs
—Providing insight into social problems by supplying information about how
   problems—such as aging, conflict, or bereavement—are dealt with in other cultures
—Interviewing people to obtain information about their attitudes, knowledge,
   and behavior
—Using statistics and computers to analyze data
—Adapting approaches used in public relations, marketing, or politics to different
   population groups
—Appraising; classifying; and cataloging rare, old, or valuable objects
—Repairing, reconstructing, and preserving cultural artifacts by selecting
   chemical treatment, temperature, humidity, and storage methods
—Drawing maps and constructing scale models
—Photographing sites, objects, people, and events
—Interpreting or translating
—Using scientific equipment and measuring devices
—Analyzing craft techniques
—Cooperating in an ethnographic or archaeological research team
—Making policy based on social science research data, problem-solving methods,
   and professional ethical standards
—Designing research projects and applying for grants
—Producing a research paper in appropriate format and style
—Orally presenting research results
—Applying a variety of ethnographic data collection techniques: ethnosemantics,
   proxemics, life histories, ethnohistory, folklore, event analysis, genealogies, etc.
—Producing and editing a scholarly journal
—Leading a pre-professional organization such as a student anthropology society
   or honors society
—Developing public relations for a museum, field project, or conference
—Designing, building, installing, and acting as docent for museum exhibits
—Coaching, instructing, tutoring, and team-teaching with peers
—Studying a second language

Source: Adapted from John T. Omohundro, *Careers in Anthropology* (Mountain View, CA: Mayfield, 1998).

What Careers Do Anthropology B.A.'s Pursue?

Students can be brought out of anthro shock by infusions of empirical data.
Surveys have been conducted to assess what work anthropology students are
prepared for and what fields alumni actually entered. In *Anthropology and
Jobs*, H. Russell Bernard and Willis Sibley identified thirteen fields that the
anthropology B.A. could enter with no additional training.[5] These included

[5]H. Russell Bernard and Willis E. Sibley, *Anthropology and Jobs: A Guide for Undergraduates*,
American Anthropological Association special publication (Washington, DC: American Anthropological Association, 1975).

TABLE 2   Résumé Language for Anthropological Abilities

Social agility—In an unfamiliar social or career-related setting, you learn to size up quickly the "rules of the game." You can become accepted more quickly than you could without anthropology.

Observation—As you must often learn about a culture from within it, you learn how to interview and observe as a participant.

Planning—You learn how to find patterns in the behavior of a cultural group. This allows you to generalize about their behavior and predict what they might do in a given situation.

Social sensitivity—While other people's ways of doing things may be different from your own, you learn the importance of events and conditions that have contributed to this difference. You also recognize that other cultures view your ways as strange. You learn the value of behaving toward others with appropriate preparation, care, and understanding.

Accuracy in interpreting behavior—You become familiar with the range of behavior in different cultures. You learn how to look at cultural causes of behavior before assigning causes yourself.

Challenging conclusions—You learn that analyses of human behavior are open to challenge. You learn how to use new knowledge to test past conclusions.

Interpreting information—You learn how to use data collected by others, reorganizing or interpreting it to reach original conclusions.

Simplifying information—As anthropology is conducted among publics as well as about them, you learn how to simplify technical information for communication to non-technical people.

Contextualizing—Attention to details is a trait of anthropology. However, you learn that any detail might not be as important as its context, and can even be misleading when context is ignored.

Problem-solving—Often functioning within a cultural group, or acting upon culturally sensitive issues, you learn to approach problems with care. Before acting, you learn how to identify the problem, set your goals, decide upon the actions you will take, and calculate possible effects on other people.

Persuasive writing—Anthropology strives to represent the behavior of one group to another group, and is in continual need of interpretation. You learn the value of bringing someone else to your view through written argument.

Social perspective—You learn how to perceive the acts of individuals and local groups as cause and effect of larger sociocultural systems. This enables you to "act locally and think globally."

Source: John T. Omohundro, *Careers in Anthropology* (Mountain View, CA: Mayfield, 1998).

journalism, police work, and the travel or tour industry. They also identified twenty-eight fields the anthropology B.A. could enter if additional training, up to the M.A. or M.S. level in the appropriate discipline, was acquired. These fields included dietetics, market research, city planning, museums, personnel, and community development, to name a few.

Ten years later, two of my students conducted a survey of anthropology alumni from 32 liberal arts colleges in the northeast U.S.[6] Of the 616 respondents,

[6]Lawrence W. Kratts and Clarissa Hunter, "Undergraduate Alumni Survey Results," *Anthropology Newsletter* (November 1986).

62% worked in the profit sector, 9% in the non-profit sector, and 6% in government. 16% were still in a graduate or professional school.

The respondents' occupations were sorted into seventeen categories. Academics accounted for 10%, some of whom were in disciplines other than anthropology, but managers ("director," "administrator," etc.) dominated at 19%. It appears that a large number of anthropology majors become actors in a bureaucracy, supervising others. Medicine, communications, and business together accounted for another 16% of respondents' current positions.

Does this range of work positions outside of anthropology, as usually conceived, signal a failure on our part to place our advisees in positions that will utilize their major? I don't think so, and neither do the alumni. 71% of the northeast alumni agreed with the statement, "my anthropology education helps me in my current work." An owner of a small business wrote, "All aspects of the [antique] business are satisfying: attending antique shows, unearthing an early item, researching its age and provenance, restoring or repairing it, and educating a potential customer about it. . . ."

Most (81%) of the alumni returning the survey claimed they were satisfied and challenged by their current work, and 74% felt their decision to major in anthropology was a good one. Some alumni waxed enthusiastic about anthropology as the foundation for a liberal arts education. A banker urged current majors, "Go for it: no one in business will ever hold a liberal arts education against you. . . . In the long run this will mark you as superior to a crowd of business students. . . ." Alumni highlighted the value in their current work of cultural relativism, examining human behavior holistically, and using qualitative research methods, all acquired in the major. A social services administrator reported, "I work as a management analyst in a county social services agency. While it is difficult to get an anthro degree recognized as relevant, the anthropological approach is, I feel, one of the best for this sort of job. I'm always translating. . . ."

More recent surveys of alumni, such as the six colleges in the North Carolina system in 1988[7] and a SUNY Plattsburgh survey in 1993,[8] produced similar results. The majority of anthropology majors are 1) glad they majored in anthropology, 2) using some or all of the skills and perspectives they acquired in the major, and 3) enjoying their work, even if few of them are hanging out shingles bearing the title "anthropologist."

Along with their satisfaction, the alumni have some complaints and some advice for current students and their teachers. Overall, alumni were disappointed with the quality and quantity of career advice they received while undergraduates. They also see now that they would have benefitted from more careful choices of electives and course work outside of anthropology.

The northeast alumni urged current students to take courses in math, statistics, communications, economics, science, and computing. This advice

[7]Stanton Tefft, with Cathy Harris and Glen Godwin, "North Carolina Undergraduate Alumni Survey," *Anthropology Newsletter* (January 1988).

[8]James Armstrong, personal communication, 1993.

matches that offered by alumni from most majors, who recommend courses in administration, writing, interpersonal relations, economics, accounting, and math. In our northeast survey, anthropology alumni also strongly urged students to gain as much practical experience as possible through field schools, lab and methods courses, senior theses, independent research projects, overseas study, and collaboration with professors' research.

Conclusion

The purpose of this essay has been to help anthropology teachers deal with anthro shock among their students. I advocate swift first aid with the easy answer, but it is essential to have the evidence to back up that answer. I also advocate cooperation with careers planning professionals. Anthropology offers many marketable skills, or good training for a variety of fields of work, but students, working within the world view of college life and transcript semantics, often don't know how to translate their abilities into ones the rest of the world wants.

Surveys of alumni show that they pursue many lines of work, enjoy their work, are using their anthropological perspective and skills, and are glad they majored in anthropology. Their self-descriptions in surveys suggest that they majored in anthropology because its fundamental concepts and methods for understanding human behavior matched their long-established dispositions. After college, they found satisfying employment in positions where those same dispositions—now more developed through the major—were welcome and useful. This led me to a self-discovery theory of liberal arts education. That is, college is not a place where the student, as a blank slate ready to become a cog, learns "what I need to know to get a job." Instead, college is a place where the student discovers "what I like to do" and then refines his or her ability to do it. I've discovered that many career planning professionals knew this all along.

In sum, the evidence is that anthropology students not only find meaningful work, but they can use their anthropology to get that work, and we teachers can use our anthropology to improve our career advising. Not every anthropologist feels comfortable giving career advice, for several reasons, some of which I sympathize with and some I don't. Not every student needs to rush from college to a career, either, but I have discussed here some ways to help them if they want to move along.

Postscript: Grebbleberry recovered and is now doing fine as a technical illustrator in Oregon, coupling her artistic ability to her love of archaeology.

Review Questions

1. According to Omohundro, what are the "hard" and "easy" answers to the question, "What can I do with an anthropology major?"

2. What is the difference between the way people in small-scale and complex societies make the transition into the world of work?

3. What does Omohundro mean by the term *transcultural presentation?*

4. List some of the skills acquired by undergraduate anthropology majors that are useful to employers. How can these be translated into résumé language that employers can understand?

5. According to available studies, in what job sectors do anthropology graduates most often find employment?

6. What advice do anthropology graduates have for anthropology programs and students?

Introduction and Review Questions reprinted from *Conformity and Conflict: Readings in Cultural Anthropology*, 12/e, Ed. James Spradley and David W. McCurdy, (2006), by permission of Allyn and Bacon.

2

Eating Christmas in the Kalahari

Richard Borshay Lee

What happens when an anthropologist living among the !Kung of Africa de-cides to be generous and to share a large animal with everyone at Christ-mastime? This compelling account of the misunderstanding and confusion that resulted takes the reader deeper into the nature of culture. Richard Lee carefully traces how the !Kung perceived his generosity and taught the an-thropologist something about his own culture.

The !Kung Bushmen's knowledge of Christmas is thirdhand. The London Missionary Society brought the holiday to the southern Tswana tribes in the early nineteenth century. Later, native catechists spread the idea far and wide among the Bantu-speaking pastoralists, even in the remotest corners of the Kalahari Desert. The Bushmen's idea of the Christmas story, stripped to its es-sentials, is "praise the birth of white man's god-chief"; what keeps their interest in the holiday high is the Tswana-Herero custom of slaughtering an ox for his

Reprinted from *Natural History,* December 1969. Copyright © 1969 by Natural History Magazine, Inc.

Bushmen neighbors as an annual goodwill gesture. Since the 1930s, part of the Bushmen's annual round of activities has included a December congregation at the cattle posts for trading, marriage brokering, and several days of trance dance feasting at which the local Tswana headman is host.

As a social anthropologist working with !Kung Bushmen, I found that the Christmas ox custom suited my purposes. I had come to the Kalahari to study the hunting and gathering subsistence economy of the !Kung, and to accomplish this it was essential not to provide them with food, share my own food, or interfere in any way with their food-gathering activities. While liberal handouts of tobacco and medical supplies were appreciated, they were scarcely adequate to erase the glaring disparity in wealth between the anthropologist, who maintained a two-month inventory of canned goods, and the Bushmen, who rarely had a day's supply of food on hand. My approach, while paying off in terms of data, left me open to frequent accusations of stinginess and hardheartedness. By their lights, I was a miser.

The Christmas ox was to be my way of saying thank you for the cooperation of the past year; and since it was to be our last Christmas in the field, I was determined to slaughter the largest, meatiest ox that money could buy, insuring that the feast and trance dance would be a success.

Through December I kept my eyes open at the wells as the cattle were brought down for watering. Several animals were offered, but none had quite the grossness that I had in mind. Then, ten days before the holiday, a Herero friend led an ox of astonishing size and mass up to our camp. It was solid black, stood five feet high at the shoulder, had a five-foot span of horns, and must have weighed 1,200 pounds on the hoof. Food consumption calculations are my specialty, and I quickly figured that bones and viscera aside, there was enough meat—at least four pounds—for every man, woman, and child of the 150 Bushmen in the vicinity of /ai/ai who were expected at the feast.

Having found the right animal at last, I paid the Herero £20 ($56) and asked him to keep the beast with his herd until Christmas day. The next morning word spread among the people that the big solid black one was the ox chosen by /ontah (my Bushman name; it means, roughly, "whitey") for the Christmas feast. That afternoon I received the first delegation. Ben!a, an outspoken sixty-year-old mother of five, came to the point slowly.

"Where were you planning to eat Christmas?"

"Right here at /ai/ai," I replied.

"Alone or with others?"

"I expect to invite all the people to eat Christmas with me."

"Eat what?"

"I have purchased Yehave's black ox, and I am going to slaughter and cook it."

"That's what we were told at the well but refused to believe it until we heard it from yourself."

"Well, it's the black one," I replied expansively, although wondering what she was driving at.

"Oh, no!" Ben!a groaned, turning to her group. "They were right." Turning back to me she asked, "Do you expect us to eat that bag of bones?"

"Bag of bones! It's the biggest ox at /ai/ai."

"Big, yes, but old. And thin. Everybody knows there's no meat on that old ox. What did you expect us to eat off it, the horns?"

Everybody chuckled at Ben!a's one-liner as they walked away, but all I could manage was a weak grin.

That evening it was the turn of the young men. They came to sit at our evening fire. /gaugo, about my age, spoke to me man-to-man.

"/ontah, you have always been square with us," he lied. "What has happened to change your heart? That sack of guts and bones of Yehave's will hardly feed one camp, let alone all the Bushmen around /ai/ai." And he proceeded to enumerate the seven camps in the /ai/ai vicinity, family by family. "Perhaps you have forgotten that we are not few, but many. Or are you too blind to tell the difference between a proper cow and an old wreck? That ox is thin to the point of death."

"Look, you guys," I retorted, "that is a beautiful animal, and I'm sure you will eat it with pleasure at Christmas."

"Of course we will eat it; it's food. But it won't fill us up to the point where we will have enough strength to dance. We will eat and go home to bed with stomachs rumbling."

That night as we turned in, I asked my wife, Nancy, "What did you think of the black ox?"

"It looked enormous to me. Why?"

"Well, about eight different people have told me I got gypped; that the ox is nothing but bones."

"What's the angle?" Nancy asked. "Did they have a better one to sell?"

"No, they just said that it was going to be a grim Christmas because there won't be enough meat to go around. Maybe I'll get an independent judge to look at the beast in the morning."

Bright and early, Halingisi, a Tswana cattle owner, appeared at our camp. But before I could ask him to give me his opinion on Yehave's black ox, he gave me the eye signal that indicated a confidential chat. We left the camp and sat down.

"/ontah, I'm surprised at you; you've lived here for three years and still haven't learned anything about cattle."

"But what else can a person do but choose the biggest, strongest animal one can find?" I retorted.

"Look, just because an animal is big doesn't mean that it has plenty of meat on it. The black one was a beauty when it was younger, but now it is thin to the point of death."

"Well, I've already bought it. What can I do at this stage?"

"Bought it already? I thought you were just considering it. Well, you'll have to kill it and serve it, I suppose. But don't expect much of a dance to follow."

My spirits dropped rapidly. I could believe that Ben!a and /gaugo just might be putting me on about the black ox, but Halingisi seemed to be an impartial critic. I went around that day feeling as though I had bought a lemon of a used car.

In the afternoon it was Tomazo's turn. Tomazo is a fine hunter, a top trance performer . . . and one of my most reliable informants. He approached the subject of the Christmas cow as part of my continuing Bushman education.

"My friend, the way it is with us Bushmen," he began, "is that we love meat. And even more than that, we love fat. When we hunt we always search for the fat ones, the ones dripping with layers of white fat: fat that turns into a clear, thick oil in the cooking pot, fat that slides down your gullet, fills your stomach and gives you a roaring diarrhea," he rhapsodized.

"So, feeling as we do," he continued, "it gives us pain to be served such a scrawny thing as Yehave's black ox. It is big, yes, and no doubt its giant bones are good for soup, but fat is what we really crave, and so we will eat Christmas this year with a heavy heart."

The prospect of a gloomy Christmas now had me worried, so I asked Tomazo what I could do about it.

"Look for a fat one, a young one . . . smaller, but fat. Fat enough to make us //gom (evacuate the bowels), then we will be happy."

My suspicions were aroused when Tomazo said that he happened to know a young, fat, barren cow that the owner was willing to part with. Was Tomazo working on commission, I wondered? But I dispelled this unworthy thought when we approached the Herero owner of the cow in question and found that he had decided not to sell.

The scrawny wreck of a Christmas ox now became the talk of the /ai/ai water hole and was the first news told to the outlying groups as they began to come in from the bush for the feast. What finally convinced me that real trouble might be brewing was the visit from u!au, an old conservative with a reputation for fierceness. His nickname meant spear and referred to an incident thirty years ago in which he had speared a man to death. He had an intense manner; fixing me with his eyes, he said in clipped tones:

"I have only just heard about the black ox today, or else I would have come here earlier. /ontah, do you honestly think you can serve meat like that to people and avoid a fight?" He paused, letting the implications sink in. "I don't mean fight you, /ontah; you are a white man. I mean a fight between Bushmen. There are many fierce ones here, and with such a small quantity of meat to distribute, how can you give everybody a fair share? Someone is sure to accuse another of taking too much or hogging all the choice pieces. Then you will see what happens when some go hungry while others eat."

The possibility of at least a serious argument struck me as all too real. I had witnessed the tension that surrounds the distribution of meat from a kudu or gemsbok kill, and had documented many arguments that sprang up from a real or imagined slight in meat distribution. The owners of a kill may spend up to two hours arranging and rearranging the piles of meat under the gaze of a circle of recipients before handing them out. And I knew that the Christmas feast at /ai/ai would be bringing together groups that had feuded in the past.

Convinced now of the gravity of the situation, I went in earnest to search for a second cow; but all my inquiries failed to turn one up.

The Christmas feast was evidently going to be a disaster, and the incessant complaints about the meagerness of the ox had already taken the fun out of it for me. Moreover, I was getting bored with the wisecracks, and after losing my temper a few times, I resolved to serve the beast anyway. If the meat fell short, the hell with it. In the Bushmen idiom, I announced to all who would listen:

"I am a poor man and blind. If I have chosen one that is too old and too thin, we will eat it anyway and see if there is enough meat there to quiet the rumbling of our stomachs."

On hearing this speech, Ben!a offered me a rare word of comfort. "It's thin," she said philosophically, "but the bones will make a good soup."

At dawn Christmas morning, instinct told me to turn over the butchering and cooking to a friend and take off with Nancy to spend Christmas alone in the bush. But curiosity kept me from retreating. I wanted to see what such a scrawny ox looked like on butchering, and if there *was* going to be a fight, I wanted to catch every word of it. Anthropologists are incurable that way.

The great beast was driven up to our dancing ground, and a shot in the forehead dropped it in its tracks. Then, freshly cut branches were heaped around the fallen carcass to receive the meat. Ten men volunteered to help with the cutting. I asked /gaugo to make the breast bone cut. This cut, which begins the butchering process for most large game, offers easy access for removal of the viscera. But it also allows the hunter to spot-check the amount of fat on an animal. A fat game animal carries a white layer up to an inch thick on the chest, while in a thin one, the knife will quickly cut to bone. All eyes fixed on his hand as /gaugo, dwarfed by the great carcass, knelt to the breast. The first cut opened a pool of solid white in the black skin. The second and third cut widened and deepened the creamy white. Still no bone. It was pure fat; it must have been two inches thick.

"Hey /gau," I burst out, "that ox is loaded with fat. What's this about the ox being too thin to bother eating? Are you out of your mind?"

"Fat?" /gau shot back. "You call that fat? This wreck is thin, sick, dead!" And he broke out laughing. So did everyone else. They rolled on the ground, paralyzed with laughter. Everybody laughed except me; I was thinking.

I ran back to the tent and burst in just as Nancy was getting up. "Hey, the black ox. It's fat as hell! They were kidding about it being too thin to eat. It was a joke or something. A put-on. Everyone is really delighted with it."

"Some joke," my wife replied. "It was so funny that you were ready to pack up and leave /ai/ai."

If it had indeed been a joke, it had been an extraordinarily convincing one, and tinged, I thought, with more than a touch of malice, as many jokes are. Nevertheless, that it was a joke lifted my spirits considerably, and I returned to the butchering site where the shape of the ox was rapidly disappearing under the axes and knives of the butchers. The atmosphere had become festive. Grinning broadly, their arms covered with blood well past the elbow, men packed chunks of meat into the big cast-iron cooking pots, fifty pounds to the load, and muttered and chuckled all the while about the thinness and worthlessness of the animal and /ontah's poor judgment.

We danced and ate that ox two days and two nights; we cooked and distributed fourteen potfuls of meat and no one went home hungry and no fights broke out.

But the "joke" stayed in my mind. I had a growing feeling that something important had happened in my relationship with the Bushmen and that the clue lay in the meaning of the joke. Several days later, when most of the people had dispersed back to the bush camps, I raised the question with Hakekgose, a Tswana man who had grown up among the !Kung, married a !Kung girl, and who probably knew their culture better than any other non-Bushman.

"With us whites," I began, "Christmas is supposed to be the day of friendship and brotherly love. What I can't figure out is why the Bushmen went to such lengths to criticize and belittle the ox I had bought for the feast. The animal was perfectly good and their jokes and wisecracks practically ruined the holiday for me."

"So it really did bother you," said Hakekgose. "Well, that's the way they always talk. When I take my rifle and go hunting with them, if I miss, they laugh at me for the rest of the day. But even if I hit and bring one down, it's no better. To them, the kill is always too small or too old or too thin; and as we sit down on the kill site to cook and eat the liver, they keep grumbling, even with their mouths full of meat. They say things like, 'Oh, this is awful! What a worthless animal! Whatever made me think that this Tswana rascal could hunt!' "

"Is this the way outsiders are treated?" I asked.

"No, it is their custom; they talk that way to each other, too. Go and ask them."

/gaugo had been one of the most enthusiastic in making me feel bad about the merit of the Christmas ox. I sought him out first.

"Why did you tell me the black ox was worthless, when you could see that it was loaded with fat and meat?"

"It is our way," he said, smiling. "We always like to fool people about that. Say there is a Bushman who has been hunting. He must not come home and announce like a braggart, 'I have killed a big one in the bush!' He must first sit down in silence until I or someone else comes up to his fire and asks, 'What did you see today?' He replies quietly, 'Ah, I'm no good for hunting. I saw nothing at all [pause] just a little tiny one.' Then I smile to myself," /gaugo continued, "because I know he has killed something big.

"In the morning we make up a party of four or five people to cut up and carry the meat back to the camp. When we arrive at the kill we examine it and cry out, 'You mean to say you have dragged us all the way out here in order to make us cart home your pile of bones? Oh, if I had known it was this thin I wouldn't have come.' Another one pipes up, 'People, to think I gave up a nice day in the shade for this. At home we may be hungry, but at least we have nice cool water to drink.' If the horns are big, someone says, 'Did you think that somehow you were going to boil down the horns for soup?'

"To all this you must respond in kind. 'I agree,' you say, 'this one is not worth the effort; let's just cook the liver for strength and leave the rest for the hyenas. It is not too late to hunt today and even a duiker or a steenbok would be better than this mess.'

"Then you set to work nevertheless; butcher the animal, carry the meat back to the camp and everyone eats," /gaugo concluded.

Things were beginning to make sense. Next, I went to Tomazo. He corroborated /gaugo's story of the obligatory insults over a kill and added a few details of his own.

"But," I asked, "why insult a man after he has gone to all that trouble to track and kill an animal and when he is going to share the meat with you so that your children will have something to eat?"

"Arrogance," was his cryptic answer.

"Arrogance?"

"Yes, when a young man kills much meat he comes to think of himself as a chief or a big man, and he thinks of the rest of us as his servants or inferiors. We can't accept this. We refuse one who boasts, for someday his pride will make him kill somebody. So we always speak of his meat as worthless. This way we cool his heart and make him gentle."

"But why didn't you tell me this before?" I asked Tomazo with some heat.

"Because you never asked me," said Tomazo, echoing the refrain that has come to haunt every field ethnographer.

The pieces now fell into place. I had known for a long time that in situations of social conflict with Bushmen I held all the cards. I was the only source of tobacco in a thousand square miles, and I was not incapable of cutting an individual off for noncooperation. Though my boycott never lasted longer than a few days, it was an indication of my strength. People resented my presence at the water hole, yet simultaneously dreaded my leaving. In short I was a perfect target for the charge of arrogance and for the Bushman tactic of enforcing humility.

I had been taught an object lesson by the Bushmen; it had come from an unexpected corner and had hurt me in a vulnerable area. For the big black ox was to be the one totally generous, unstinting act of my year at /ai/ai and I was quite unprepared for the reaction I received.

As I read it, their message was this: There are no totally generous acts. All "acts" have an element of calculation. One black ox slaughtered at Christmas does not wipe out a year of careful manipulation of gifts given to serve your own ends. After all, to kill an animal and share the meat with people is really no more than the Bushmen do for each other every day and with far less fanfare.

In the end, I had to admire how the Bushmen had played out the farce—collectively straight-faced to the end. Curiously, the episode reminded me of the *Good Soldier Schweik* and his marvelous encounters with authority. Like Schweik, the Bushmen had retained a thoroughgoing skepticism of good intentions. Was it this independence of spirit, I wondered, that had kept them culturally viable in the face of generations of contact with more powerful societies, both black and white? The thought that the Bushmen were alive and well in the

Kalahari was strangely comforting. Perhaps, armed with that independence and with their superb knowledge of their environment, they might yet survive the future.

Review Questions

1. What was the basis of the misunderstanding experienced by Lee when he gave an ox for the Christmas feast held by the !Kung?

2. Construct a model of cross-cultural misunderstanding, using the information presented by Lee in this article.

3. Why do you think the !Kung ridicule and denigrate people who have been successful hunters or who have provided them with a Christmas ox? Why do Americans expect people to be grateful to receive gifts?

Introduction and Review Questions reprinted from *Conformity and Conflict: Readings in Cultural Anthropology*, 12/e, Ed. James Spradley and David W. McCurdy, (2006), by permission of Allyn and Bacon.

3

Office Work and the Crack Alternative

Philippe Bourgois

Market economies are standard features of most countries in today's world. Almost everywhere, there is a formal market economy identified by visible, legal, organized economic structures and activities, which economists attempt to measure and governments can tax and regulate. Banks, factories, corporations, retail outlets—these and other publicly organized economic units are usually part of the formal economy.

But underneath the formal economy lies an informal system often called the shadow *or* underground *economy. The shadow economy is usually small-scale, personal, and at times illegal. Governments find it difficult to tax and regulate the shadow economy. Yet it is the shadow economy that provides a living for hundreds of millions of largely poor men and women around the world today.*

In this article, Philippe Bourgois focuses on part of the shadow economy in the United States, the illegal sale of crack by Puerto Rican immigrants

Reprinted from *Urban Life: Readings in the Anthropology of the City,* Fourth Edition, edited by George Gmelch and Walter P. Zenner (2002), Waveland Press, Inc.

in New York City. He argues that the loss of manufacturing jobs in New York is a key to understanding the rise of drug dealing in Spanish Harlem. Manufacturing jobs once provided dignified and stable employment for poorly educated, unskilled Puerto Rican men and women. As factories closed during the 1960s, '70s, and '80s, the unemployed could find work only in service industries such as security corporations, law firms, and insurance companies. Because they were uneducated and culturally different, they could hold only minimum wage jobs in such worlds, as they are usually controlled by educated, largely Anglo people who openly look down on them. In the end, they could achieve higher status and often higher income in their own ethnic community by dealing drugs. The result has been a destructive spiral into addiction, murder, and prison. Bourgois concludes the article with an addendum noting that high employment in the late 1990s provided more work opportunities for Puerto Ricans in the formal economy and that crack dealing has largely given way to the less visible sale of marijuana and heroin.

For a total of approximately three and a half years during the late 1980s and early 1990s, I lived with my wife and young son in an irregularly heated, rat-filled tenement in East Harlem, New York. This two-hundred-square-block neighborhood—better known locally as *El Barrio* or Spanish Harlem—is visibly impoverished yet it is located in the heart of New York, the richest city in the Western Hemisphere. It is literally a stone's throw from multimillion-dollar condominiums. Although one in three families survived on some form of public assistance in 1990, the majority of El Barrio's 110,600 Puerto Rican and African-American residents fall into the ranks of the working poor.[1] They eke out an uneasy subsistence in entry-level service and manufacturing jobs in one of the most expensive cities in the world.

The public sector (e.g., the police, social welfare agencies, the Sanitation Department) has broken down in El Barrio and does not function effectively. This has caused the legally employed residents of the neighborhood to lose control of their streets and public spaces to the drug economy. My tenement's block was not atypical and within a few hundred yards' radius I could obtain heroin, crack, powder cocaine, hypodermic needles, methadone, Valium, angel dust, marijuana, mescaline, bootleg alcohol, and tobacco. Within two hundred feet of my stoop there were three competing crack houses selling vials at two, three, and five dollars. Several doctors operated "pill mills" on the blocks around me,

---

[1]According to the 1990 Census, in East Harlem 48.3 percent of males and 35.2 percent of females over sixteen were officially reported as employed—compared to a citywide average of 64.3 percent for men and 49 percent for women. Another 10.4 percent of the men and 5.7 percent of the women in East Harlem were actively looking for legal work. . . . In El Barrio as a whole, 60 percent of all households reported legally earned incomes. Twenty-six percent received Public Assistance, 6.3 percent received Supplemental Security Income, and 5 percent received Medicaid benefits.

writing prescriptions for opiates and barbiturates upon demand. In the projects within view of my living-room window, the Housing Authority police arrested a fifty-five-year-old mother and her twenty-two-year-old daughter while they were "bagging" twenty-two pounds of cocaine into ten-dollar quarter-gram "Jumbo" vials of adulterated product worth over a million dollars on the streets. The police found twenty-five thousand dollars in cash in small-denomination bills in this same apartment.[2] In other words, there are millions of dollars' worth of business going on directly in front of the youths growing up in East Harlem tenements and housing projects. Why should these young men and women take the subway downtown to work minimum-wage jobs—or even double minimum-wage jobs—in downtown offices when they can usually earn more, at least in the short run, by selling drugs on the street corner in front of their apartment or schoolyard?

This dynamic underground economy is predicated on violence and substance abuse. It has spawned what I call a "street culture" of resistance and self-destruction. The central concern of my study is the relationship of street culture to the worlds of work accessible to street dealers—that is, the legal and illegal labor markets that employ them and give meaning to their lives. I hope to show the local-level implications of the global-level restructuring of the U.S. economy away from factory production and toward services. In the process, I have recorded the words and experiences of some unrepentant victims who are part of a network of some twenty-five street-level crack dealers operating on and around my block. To summarize, I am arguing that the transformation from manufacturing to service employment—especially in the professional office work setting—is much more culturally disruptive than the already revealing statistics on reductions in income, employment, unionization, and worker's benefits would indicate. Low-level service sector employment engenders a humiliating ideological—or cultural—confrontation between a powerful corps of white office executives and their assistants versus a younger generation of poorly educated, alienated, "colored" workers. It also often takes the form of a sharply polarized confrontation over gender roles.

Shattered Working-Class Dreams

All the crack dealers and addicts whom I have interviewed had worked at one or more legal jobs in their early youth. In fact, most entered the labor market at a younger age than the typical American. Before they were twelve years old they were bagging groceries at the supermarket for tips, stocking beers off-the-books in local *bodegas,* or shining shoes. For example, Primo, the night manager at a video game arcade that sells five-dollar vials of crack on the block where I lived, pursued a traditional working-class dream in his early

[2]Both of these police actions were reported in the local print and television media, but I am withholding the cities to protect the anonymity of my street address.

adolescence. With the support of his extended kin who were all immersed in a working-class "common sense," he dropped out of junior high school to work in a local garment factory:

> I was like fourteen or fifteen playing hooky and pressing dresses and whatever they were making on the steamer. They was cheap, cheap clothes.
>
> My mother's sister was working there first and then her son, my cousin Willie—the one who's in jail now—was the one they hired first, because his mother agreed: "If you don't want to go to school, you gotta work."
>
> So I started hanging out with him. I wasn't planning on working in the factory. I was supposed to be in school; but it just sort of happened.

Ironically, young Primo actually became the agent who physically moved the factory out of the inner city. In the process, he became merely one more of the 445,900 manufacturing workers in New York City who lost their jobs as factory employment dropped 50 percent from 1963 to 1983 . . .

Almost all the crack dealers had similar tales of former factory jobs. For poor adolescents, the decision to drop out of school and become a marginal factory worker is attractive. It provides the employed youth with access to the childhood "necessities"—sneakers, basketballs, store-bought snacks—that sixteen-year-olds who stay in school cannot afford. In the descriptions of their first forays into legal factory-based employment, one hears clearly the extent to which they, and their families, subscribed to mainstream working-class ideologies about the dignity of engaging in "hard work" rather than education.

Had these enterprising, early-adolescent workers from El Barrio not been confined to the weakest sector of manufacturing in a period of rapid job loss, their teenage working-class dreams might have stabilized. Instead, upon reaching their mid-twenties, they discovered themselves to be unemployable high school dropouts. This painful realization of social marginalization expresses itself across a generational divide. The parents and grandparents of the dealers continue to maintain working-class values of honesty and hard work which conflict violently with the reality of their children's immersion in street culture. They are constantly accused of slothfulness by their mothers and even by friends who have managed to maintain legal jobs. They do not have a regional perspective on the dearth of adequate entry-level jobs available to "functional illiterates" in New York, and they begin to suspect that they might indeed be "*vago bons*" [lazy bums] who do not *want* to work hard and cannot help themselves. Confused, they take refuge in an alternative search for career, meaning, and ecstasy in substance abuse.

Formerly, when most entry-level jobs were found in factories, the contradiction between an oppositional street culture and traditional working-class, masculine, shop-floor culture was less pronounced—especially when the work site was protected by a union. Factories are inevitably rife with confrontational hierarchies. Nevertheless, on the shop-floor, surrounded by older union workers, high school dropouts who are well versed in the latest and toughest street culture styles function effectively. In the factory, being tough and violently macho has high cultural value; a certain degree of opposition to the foreman and the "bossman" is expected and is considered appropriate.

In contrast, this same oppositional street-identity is nonfunctional in the professional office worker service sector that has burgeoned in New York's high-finance-driven economy. It does not allow for the humble, obedient, social interaction—often across gender lines—that professional office workers routinely impose on their subordinates. A qualitative change has occurred, therefore, in the tenor of social interaction in office-based employment. Workers in a mail room or behind a photocopy machine cannot publicly maintain their cultural autonomy. Most concretely, they have no union; more subtly, there are few fellow workers surrounding them to insulate them and to provide them with a culturally based sense of class solidarity.[3] Instead they are besieged by supervisors and bosses from an alien, hostile, and obviously dominant culture who ridicule street culture. Workers like Primo appear inarticulate to their professional supervisors when they try to imitate the language of power in the workplace and instead stumble pathetically over the enunciation of unfamiliar words. They cannot decipher the hastily scribbled instructions—rife with mysterious abbreviations—that are left for them by harried office managers. The "common sense" of white-collar work is foreign to them; they do not, for example, understand the logic for filing triplicate copies of memos or for postdating invoices. When they attempt to improvise or show initiative they fail miserably and instead appear inefficient, or even hostile, for failing to follow "clearly specified" instructions.

Their "social skills" are even more inadequate than their limited professional capacities. They do not know how to look at their fellow co-service workers, let alone their supervisors, without intimidating them. They cannot walk down the hallway to the water fountain without unconsciously swaying their shoulders aggressively as if patrolling their home turf. Gender barriers are an even more culturally charged realm. They are repeatedly reprimanded for harassing female coworkers.

The cultural clash between white "yuppie" power and inner-city "scrambling jive" in the service sector is much more than a superficial question of style. It is about access to power. Service workers who are incapable of obeying the rules of interpersonal interaction dictated by professional office culture will never be upwardly mobile. Their supervisors will think they are dumb or have a "bad attitude." Once again, a gender dynamic exacerbates the confusion and sense of insult experienced by young, male inner-city employees because most supervisors in the lowest reaches of the service sector are women. Street culture does not allow males to be subordinate across gender lines.

---

[3]Significantly, there are subsectors of the service industry that are relatively unionized—such as hospital and custodial work—where there is a limited autonomous space for street culture and working-class resistance.

"Gettin' Dissed"

On the street, the trauma of experiencing a threat to one's personal dignity has been frozen linguistically in the commonly used phrase "to diss," which is short for "to disrespect." Significantly, one generation ago ethnographers working in rural Puerto Rico specifically noted the importance of the traditional Puerto Rican concept of *respeto* in mediating labor relations:

> The good owner "respects" (*respeta*) the laborer. . . . It is probably to the interest of the landowner to make concessions to his best workers, to deal with them on a respect basis, and to enmesh them in a network of mutual obligations.[4]

Puerto Rican street-dealers do not find respect in the entry-level service sector jobs that have increased two-fold in New York's economy since the 1950s. On the contrary, they "get dissed" in the new jobs that are available to them. Primo, for example, remembers the humiliation of his former work experiences as an "office boy," and he speaks of them in a race- and gender-charged idiom:

> I had a prejudiced boss. She was a fucking "ho'," Gloria. She was white. Her name was Christian. No, not Christian, Kirschman. I don't know if she was Jewish or not. When she was talking to people she would say, "He's illiterate."
>
> So what I did one day was, I just looked up the word, "illiterate," in the dictionary and I saw that she's saying to her associates that I'm stupid or something! Well, I am illiterate anyway.

The most profound dimension of Primo's humiliation was being obliged to look up in the dictionary the word used to insult him. In contrast, in the underground economy, he is sheltered from this kind of threat:

> Rocky [the crack house franchise owner] he would never disrespect me that way. He wouldn't tell me that because he's illiterate too. Plus I've got more education than him. I got a GED. . . .

Primo excels in the street's underground economy. His very persona inspires fear and respect. In contrast, in order to succeed in his former office job, Primo would have had to self-consciously alter his street identity and mimic the professional cultural style that office managers require of their subordinates and colleagues. Primo refused to accept his boss's insults and he was unable to imitate her interactional styles. He was doomed, consequently, to a marginal position behind a photocopy machine or at the mail meter. Behavior considered appropriate in street culture is considered dysfunctional in office settings.

---

[4]Eric Wolf, "San Jose: Subcultures of a 'Traditional' Coffee Municipality," in Julian Stewart (ed.), *The People of Puerto Rico* (Chicago: University of Chicago Press, 1956), p. 235.

In other words, job requirements in the service sector are largely cultural style and this conjugates powerfully with racism.

> I wouldn't have mind that she said I was illiterate. What bothered me was that when she called on the telephone, she wouldn't want me to answer even if my supervisor who was the receptionist was not there. [Note how Primo is so low in the office hierarchy that his immediate supervisor is a receptionist.]
>
> When she hears my voice it sounds like she's going to get a heart attack. She'd go, "Why are you answering the phones?"
>
> That bitch just didn't like my Puerto Rican accent.

Primo's manner of resisting this insult to his cultural dignity exacerbated his marginal position in the labor hierarchy:

> And then, when I did pick up the phone, I used to just sound *Porta'rrrican* on purpose.

In contrast to the old factory sweatshop positions, these just-above-minimum-wage office jobs require intense interpersonal contact with the middle and upper-middle classes. Close contact across class lines and the absence of a working-class autonomous space for eight hours a day in the office can be a claustrophobic experience for an otherwise ambitious, energetic, young, inner-city worker.

Caesar, who worked for Primo as lookout and bodyguard at the crack house, interpreted this requirement to obey white, middle-class norms as an affront to his dignity that specifically challenged his definition of masculinity:

> I had a few jobs like that [referring to Primo's "telephone diss"] where you gotta take a lot of shit from bitches and be a wimp.
>
> I didn't like it but I kept on working, because "Fuck it!" you don't want to fuck up the relationship. So you just be a punk [shrugging his shoulders dejectedly].

One alternative for surviving at a workplace that does not tolerate a street-based cultural identity is to become bicultural: to play politely by "the white woman's" rules downtown only to come home and revert to street culture within the safety of one's tenement or housing project at night. Tens of thousands of East Harlem residents manage this tightrope, but it often engenders accusations of betrayal and internalized racism on the part of neighbors and childhood friends who do not have—or do not want—these bicultural skills.

This is the case, for example, of Ray, a rival crack dealer whose tough street demeanor conflates with his black skin to "disqualify" him from legal office work. He quit a "nickel-and-dime messenger job downtown" in order to sell crack full time in his project stairway shortly after a white woman fled from him shrieking down the hallway of a high-rise office building. Ray and the terrified woman had ridden the elevator together, and, coincidentally, Ray had stepped off on the same floor as her to make a delivery. Worse yet, Ray had been trying to act like a "debonair male" and suspected the contradiction between his inadequate appearance and his chivalric intentions was responsible for the woman's terror:

> You know how you let a woman go off the elevator first? Well that's what I did to her but I may have looked a little shabby on the ends. Sometime my hair not combed. You know. So I could look a little sloppy to her maybe when I let her off first.

What Ray did not quite admit until I probed further is that he too had been intimidated by the lone white woman. He had been so disoriented by her taboo, unsupervised proximity that he had forgotten to press the elevator button when he originally stepped on after her:

> She went in the elevator first but then she just waits there to see what floor I press. She's playing like she don't know what floor she wants to go to because she wants to wait for me to press my floor. And I'm standing there and I forgot to press the button. I'm thinking about something else—I don't know what was the matter with me. And she's thinking like, "He's not pressing the button; I guess he's following me!"

As a crack dealer, Ray no longer has to confront this kind of confusing humiliation. Instead, he can righteously condemn his "successful" neighbors who work downtown for being ashamed of who they were born to be:

> When you see someone go downtown and get a good job, if they be Puerto Rican, you see them fix up their hair and put some contact lens in their eyes. Then they fit in. And they do it! I seen it.
>
> They turn-overs. They people who want to be white. Man, if you call them in Spanish, it wind up a problem.
>
> When they get nice jobs like that, all of a sudden, you know, they start talking proper.

Self-Destructive Resistance

During the 1980s, the real value of the minimum wage for legally employed workers declined by one-third. At the same time, social services were cut. The federal government, for example, decreased the proportion of its contribution to New York City's budget by over 50 percent . . . The breakdown of the inner city's public sector is no longer an economic threat to the expansion of New York's economy because the native-born labor force it shelters is increasingly irrelevant.

New immigrants arrive every day, and they are fully prepared to work hard for low wages under unsavory conditions. Like the parents and grandparents of Primo and Caesar, many of New York's newest immigrants are from isolated rural communities or squalid shanty towns where meat is eaten only once a week and there is no running water or electricity. Half a century ago Primo's mother fled precisely the same living conditions these new immigrants are only just struggling to escape. Her reminiscences about childhood in her natal village reveal the time warp of improved material conditions, cultural dislocation, and crushed working-class dreams that is propelling her second-generation son into a destructive street culture:

> I loved that life in Puerto Rico, because it was a healthy, healthy, healthy life.
>
> We always ate because my father always had work, and in those days the custom was to have a garden in your patio to grow food and everything that you ate.
>
> We only ate meat on Sundays because everything was cultivated on the same little parcel of land. We didn't have a refrigerator, so we ate *bacalao* [salted codfish], which can stay outside and a meat that they call *carne de vieja* [shredded beef], and sardines from a can. But thanks to God, we never felt hunger. My mother made a lot of cornflour.
>
> Some people have done better by coming here, but many people haven't. Even people from my barrio, who came trying to find a better life [*buen ambiente*] just found disaster. Married couples right from my neighborhood came only to have the husband run off with another woman.
>
> In those days in Puerto Rico, when we were in poverty, life was better. Everyone will tell you life was healthier and you could trust people. Now you can't trust anybody.
>
> What I like best was that we kept all our traditions . . . our feasts. In my village, everyone was either an Uncle or an Aunt. And when you walked by someone older, you had to ask for their blessing. It was respect. There was a lot of respect in those days [original quote in Spanish].

The Jewish and Italian-American white workers that Primo's mother replaced a generation ago when she came to New York City in hope of building a better future for her children were largely absorbed into an expanding economy that allowed them to be upwardly mobile. New York's economy always suffered periodic fluctuations, such as during the Great Depression, but those difficult periods were always temporary. The overall trend was one of economic growth. Primo's generation has not been so lucky. The contemporary economy does not particularly need them, and ethnic discrimination and cultural barriers overwhelm them whenever they attempt to work legally and seek service-sector jobs. Worse yet, an extraordinarily dynamic underground drug economy beckons them.

Rather than bemoaning the structural adjustment which is destroying their capacity to survive on legal wages, streetbound Puerto Rican youths celebrate their "decision" to bank on the underground economy and to cultivate their street identities. Caesar and Primo repeatedly assert their pride in their street careers. For example, one Saturday night after they finished their midnight shift at the crack house, I accompanied them on their way to purchase "*El*

Sapo Verde" [The Green Toad], a twenty-dollar bag of powder cocaine sold by a new company three blocks away. While waiting for Primo and Caesar to be "served" by the coke seller a few yards away, I engaged three undocumented Mexican men drinking beer on a neighboring stoop in a conversation about finding work in New York. One of the new immigrants was already earning five hundred dollars a week fixing deep-fat-fry machines. He had a straightforward racist explanation for why Caesar—who was standing next to me—was "unemployed":

> OK, OK, I'll explain it to you in one word: Because the Puerto Ricans are brutes! [Pointing at Caesar] Brutes! Do you understand?
>
> Puerto Ricans like to make easy money. They like to leech off of other people. But not us Mexicans! No way! We like to work for our money. We don't steal. We came here to work and that's all [original quote in Spanish].

Instead of physically assaulting the employed immigrant for insulting him, Caesar embraced the racist tirade, ironically turning it into the basis for a new, generational-based, "American-born," urban cultural pride. In fact, in his response, he ridicules what he interprets to be the hillbilly naiveté of the Mexicans who still believe in the "American Dream." He spoke slowly in street-English as if to mark sarcastically the contrast between his "savvy" Nuyorican (New York-born Puerto Rican) identity versus the limited English proficiency of his detractor:

> That's right, m'a man! We is real vermin lunatics that sell drugs. We don't want no part of society. "Fight the Power!"[5]
>
> What do we wanna be working for? We rather live off the system. Gain weight, lay women.
>
> When we was younger, we used to break our asses too [gesturing towards the Mexican men who were straining to understand his English]. I had all kinds of stupid jobs too . . . advertising agencies . . . computers.
>
> But not no more! Now we're in a rebellious stage. We rather evade taxes, make quick money, and just survive. But we're not satisfied with that either. Ha!

Conclusion: Ethnography and Oppression

The underground economy and the social relations thriving off of it are best understood as modes of resistance to subordination in the service sector of the new U.S. economy. This resistance, however, results in individual self destruction and wider community devastation through substance abuse and violence. This complex and contradictory dynamic whereby resistance leads to self-destruction in the inner city is difficult to convey to readers in a clear and re-

---

[5]"Fight the Power" is a rap song composed in 1990 by the African-American group, Public Enemy.

sponsible manner. Mainstream society's "common sense" understanding of so-cial stratification around ethnicity and class assumes the existence of racial hi-erarchies and blames individual victims for their failures. This makes it difficult to present ethnographic data from inner-city streets without falling prey to a "pornography of violence" or a racist voyeurism.

The public is not persuaded by a structural economic understanding of Caesar and Primo's "self-destruction." Even the victims themselves psychologize their unsatisfactory lives. Similarly, politicians and, more broadly, public policy ignore the fundamental structural economic facts of marginalization in America. Instead the first priority of federal and local social "welfare" agencies is to change the psychological—or at best the "cultural"—orientations of misguided individuals . . . U.S. politicians furiously debate family values while multi-national corporations establish global free-trade zones and unionized factory employment in the U.S. continues to disappear as overseas sweatshops multiply. Social science researchers, meanwhile, have remained silent for the most part. They politely ignore the urgent social problems engulfing the urban United States. The few marginal academic publications that do address issues of poverty and racism are easily ignored by the media and mainstream society. . . .

Epilogue

In the six years since this article was first published, four major dynamics have altered the tenor of daily life on the streets of East Harlem and have deeply af-fected the lives of the crack dealers and their families depicted in these pages: (1) the U.S. economy entered the most prolonged period of sustained growth in its recorded history, (2) the size of the Mexican immigrant population in New York City and especially in East Harlem increased dramatically, (3) the War on Drugs escalated into a quasi-official public policy of criminalizing and incar-cerating the poor and the socially marginal, and (4) drug fashion trends among inner-city youth rendered marijuana even more popular and crack and heroin even less popular among Latinos and African Americans.

Crack, cocaine, and heroin are still all sold on the block where I lived, but they are sold less visibly by a smaller number of people. It is still easy to pur-chase narcotics throughout East Harlem, but much of the drug dealing has moved indoors, out of sight, dealers no longer shouting out the brand names of their drugs. Most importantly, heroin and crack continue to be spurned by Latino and African-American youth who have seen the ravages those drugs committed on the older generations in their community. Nevertheless, in the U.S. inner city there remains an aging hardcore cohort of addicts. In most large cities crack is most visibly ensconced in predominantly African-American neighborhoods on the poorest blocks, often surrounding large public housing projects. In New York City, Puerto Rican households also continue to be at the epicenter of this ongoing, but now more self-contained, stationary cyclone of crack consumption.

In contrast to crack, heroin consumption has increased. Throughout most of the United States, heroin is cheaper and purer than in the early 1990s, belying any claims that the War on Drugs is winnable. Heroin's new appeal, however, is primarily among younger whites outside the ghetto for whom crack was never a drug of choice. It is not a drug of choice among Latino and African-American youth.

To summarize, both heroin and crack continue to be part of a multi-billion-dollar business that ravages inner-city families with special virulence. The younger generations of East Harlem residents, however, are more involved as sellers rather than consumers. Those Latino and African-American youth who do use crack or heroin generally try to hide the fact from their friends.

More important than changing drug-consumption fashions or the posturing of politicians over drug war campaigns has been the dramatic long-term improvement in the U.S. economy resulting in record low rates of unemployment. Somewhat to my surprise, some of the crack dealers and their families have benefited from this sustained economic growth. Slightly less than half have been allowed to enter the lower echelons of the legal labor market. For example, during the summer of 2000: one dealer was a unionized doorman, another was a home health care attendant, another was a plumber's assistant, three others were construction workers for small-time unlicensed contractors, and one was a cashier in a discount tourist souvenir store. Three or four of the dealers were still selling drugs, but most of them tended to be selling marijuana instead of crack or heroin. Three other dealers were in prison with long-term sentences and ironically were probably employed at well below minimum wage in the United States' burgeoning prison-based manufacturing sector. In short, the dramatic improvement in the U.S. economy has forced employers and unions to integrate more formally marginalized Puerto Ricans and African Americans into the labor market than was the case in the late 1980s and early 1990s when the research for this [article] was conducted. Nevertheless, even at the height of the growth in the U.S. economy in the year 2000, a large sector of street youth found themselves excluded. These marginals have become almost completely superfluous to the legal economy; they remain enmeshed in a still-lucrative drug economy, a burgeoning prison system, and a quagmire of chronic substance abuse. From a long-term political and economic perspective, the future does not bode well for inner-city poor of New York. In the year 2000, the United States had the largest disparity between rich and poor of any industrialized nation in the world—and this gap was not decreasing.

Review Questions

1. What kinds of jobs in the formal economy could Puerto Ricans living in East Harlem hold forty years ago? How did these jobs enable the men to preserve respect as it was defined in their culture?

2. What kinds of jobs are currently available to Puerto Rican men in New York's service economy? How do these jobs challenge the men's self-respect?

3. What structural changes in New York's formal economy have changed over the past forty years? How have these changes affected the lives of young men living in Spanish Harlem?

4. Why do Puerto Rican men take pride in their street identities?

5. Why does Bourgois claim that the Puerto Rican men's resistance to work in the legal economy leads to "self-destruction" and "wider community devastation"?

Introduction and Review Questions reprinted from *Conformity and Conflict: Readings in Cultural Anthropology*, 12/e, Ed. James Spradley and David W. McCurdy, (2006), by permission of Allyn and Bacon.

4

The Sapir-Whorf Hypothesis: Worlds Shaped by Words

David S. Thomson

For many people, language mirrors reality. Words are labels for what we sense; they record what is already there. This view, which is another manifestation of what we have called naive realism, *is clearly challenged by previous selections in this book. Members of different societies may not share cultural categories; words from one language often cannot be translated directly into another. In the 1930s, a young linguist named Benjamin Lee Whorf took the objection to the "words label reality" assertion one step further by arguing that words and grammatical structure actually shape reality. This piece by David Thomson describes Whorf's theory, shows how linguists have evaluated it, and applies it in modified form to the use of words, euphemisms, and doublespeak in the modern United States.*

Reprinted from *Human Behavior: Language* (1975), Time Life Books. Copyright © 1975 by Time-Life Books, Inc.

The scene is the storage room at a chemical plant. The time is evening. A night watchman enters the room and notes that it is partially filled with gasoline drums. The drums are in a section of the room where a sign says "Empty Barrels." The watchman lights a cigarette and throws the still-hot match into one of the empty barrels.

The result: an explosion.

The immediate cause of the explosion, of course, was the gasoline fumes that remained in the barrels. But it could be argued that a second cause of the explosion was the English language. The barrels were empty of their original contents and so belonged under the empty sign. Yet they were not empty of everything—the fumes were still present. English has no word—no single term—that can convey such a situation. Containers in English are either empty or they are not; there is no word describing the ambiguous state of being empty and yet not empty. There is no term in the language for "empty but not quite" or "empty of original contents but with something left over." There being no word for such an in-between state, it did not occur to the watchman to think of the explosive fumes.

This incident is hypothetical, but the questions about language it raises are real. The example of the gasoline drums often was cited by Benjamin Lee Whorf to illustrate a revolutionary theory he had about language. Whorf was an unusual man who combined two careers, for he was both a successful insurance executive and a brilliant (and largely self-taught) linguistic scholar. Language, he claimed, may be shaped by the world, but it in turn shapes the world. He reasoned that people can think about only those things that their language can describe or express. Without the words or structures with which to articulate a concept, that concept will not occur. To turn the proposition around, if a language is rich in ways to express certain sorts of ideas, then the speakers of that language will habitually think along those linguistic paths. In short, the language that humans speak governs their view of reality; it determines their perception of the world. The picture of the universe shifts from tongue to tongue.

The originator of this startling notion came from an intellectually active New England family. Whorf's brother John became an artist of note and his brother Richard a consummately professional actor. Benjamin's early bent was not for drawing or acting but photography, especially the chemistry that was involved in developing pictures, and this interest may have influenced his choice of the Massachusetts Institute of Technology, where he majored in chemical engineering. After he was graduated from M.I.T. he became a specialist in fire prevention and in 1919 went to work for the Hartford Fire Insurance Company. His job was to inspect manufacturing plants, particularly chemical plants, that the Hartford insured to determine whether they were safe and thus good insurance risks. He quickly became highly skilled at his work. "In no time at all," wrote C. S. Kremer, then the Hartford's board chairman, "he became in my opinion as thorough and fast a fire prevention inspector as there ever has been."

Whorf was a particularly acute chemical engineer. On one occasion he was refused admittance to inspect a client's building because, a company official maintained, a secret process was in use here. "You are making such-and-such a product?" asked Whorf. "Yes," said the official. Whorf pulled out a pad and scribbled the formula of the supposedly secret process, adding coolly, "You couldn't do it any other way." Needless to say, he was allowed to inspect the building. Whorf rose in the Hartford hierarchy to the post of assistant secretary of the company in 1940. But then in 1941 his health, never strong, gave way, and he died at the early age of forty-four.

While Whorf was becoming a successful insurance executive, he was also doing his revolutionary work in linguistics. He started by studying Hebrew but then switched to Aztec and other related languages of Mexico. Later he deciphered Maya inscriptions, and tried to reconstruct the long-lost language of the ancient Maya people of Mexico and Central America. Finally he tackled the complexities of the still-living language of the Hopi Indians of Arizona. He published his findings in respected anthropological and linguistic journals, earning the praise and respect of scholars in the two fields—all without formal training in linguistic science. As his fame as a linguist spread, the Hartford obligingly afforded him vacations and leaves to travel to the Southwest in pursuit of the structure and lexicon of the Hopi. He also put in countless hours in the Watkinson Library in Connecticut, a rich repository of Mexican and Indian lore.

It was primarily his study of Hopi that impelled Whorf toward his revolutionary ideas. He was encouraged and aided by the great cultural anthropologist and linguist of Yale, Edward Sapir, and the idea that language influences a person's view of the world is generally known as the Sapir-Whorf hypothesis. Whorf formulated it a number of times, but perhaps his clearest statement comes from his 1940 essay "Science and Linguistics": "The background linguistic system (in other words, the grammar) of each language is not merely a reproducing instrument for voicing ideas but rather is itself the shaper of ideas. . . . We dissect nature along lines laid down by our native language. The categories and types that we isolate from the world of phenomena we do not find there because they stare every observer in the face; on the contrary, the world is presented in a kaleidoscopic flux of impressions which has to be organized by our minds—and this means largely by the linguistic systems in our minds."

These ideas developed from Whorf's study of the Hopi language. He discovered that it differs dramatically from languages of the Indo-European family such as English or French, particularly in its expression of the concept of time. English and its related languages have three major tenses—past, present, and future ("it was," "it is," "it will be")—plus the fancier compound tenses such as "it will have been." Having these tenses, Whorf argued, encourages Europeans and Americans to think of time as so many ducks in a row. Time past is made up of uniform units of time—days, weeks, months, years—and the future is similarly measured out. This division of time is essentially artificial, Whorf said, since people can only experience the present. Past and future are only abstractions, but Westerners think of them as real because their language virtually forces them to do so. This view of time has given rise to the fondness in Western cultures for diaries, records, annals, histories, clocks, calendars, wages paid by the hour or day, and elaborate timetables for the use of future time. Time is continually quantified. If Westerners set out to build a house they establish a deadline; the work will be completed at a specified time in the future, such as May 5 or October 15.

Hopis do not behave this way; when they start to weave a mat they are not concerned about when it will be completed. They work on it desultorily, then quit, then begin again; the finished product may take weeks. This casual progress is not laziness but a result of the Hopi's view of time—one symptom of the fact that their language does not have the past, present, and future tenses. Instead it possesses two modes of thought: the objective, that is, things that exist now, and the subjective, things that can be thought about and therefore belong to a state of becoming. Things do not become in terms of a future measured off in days, weeks, months. Each thing that is becoming has its own individual life rhythms, growing or declining or changing in much the same manner as a plant grows, according to its inner nature. The essence of Hopi life, therefore, Whorf said, is preparing in the present so that those things that are capable of becoming can in fact come to pass. Thus weaving a mat is preparing a mat to become a mat; it will reach that state when its nature so ordains— whenever that will be.

This view of the future is understandable, Whorf noted, in an agricultural people whose welfare depends on the proper preparing of earth and seeds and plants for the hoped-for harvest. It also helps explain why the Hopi have such elaborate festivals, rituals, dances, and magic ceremonies: All are intended to aid in the mental preparation that is so necessary if the crops, which the Hopi believe to be influenced by human thought, are to grow properly. This preparing involves "much visible activity," Whorf said, "introductory formalities, preparing of special food . . . intensive sustained muscular activity like running, racing, dancing, which is thought to increase the intensity of development of events (such as growth of crops), mimetic and other magic preparations based on esoteric theory involving perhaps occult instruments like prayer sticks, prayer feathers, and prayer meal, and finally the great cyclic ceremonies and dances, which have the significance of preparing rain and crops." Whorf went on to note that the very noun for *crop* is derived from the verb that means "to prepare." *Crop* therefore is in the Hopi language literally "the prepared." Further, the Hopi prayer pipe, which is smoked as an aid in concentrating good thoughts on the growing fields of corn and wheat, is named *na'twanpi,* "instrument of preparing."

The past to the Hopi, Whorf believed, is also different from the chronological time sense of the speakers of Indo-European languages. The past is not a uniform row of days or weeks to the Hopi. It is rather an undifferentiated stream in which many deeds were done that have accumulated and prepared the present and will continue to prepare the becoming that is ahead. Everything is connected, everything accumulates. The past is not a series of events, separated and completed, but is present in the present.

To Whorf these striking differences in the Hopi language and sense of time implied that the Hopi live almost literally in another world from the speakers of Indo-European languages. The Hopi language grew out of its speakers' peculiar circumstances: As a geographically isolated agricultural people in a land where rainfall was scanty, they did the same things and prayed the same prayers year after year and thus did not need to have past and future tenses. But the language, once it had developed, perpetuated their particular and seemingly very different world view.

Many linguists and anthropologists who have worked with American Indians of the Southwest have been convinced that Whorf's theories are by and large correct. Other linguists are not convinced, however, and through the years since Whorf's death they have attacked his proposals. The controversy is unlikely to be settled soon, if ever. One of the problems is the difficulty of setting up an experiment that would either prove or disprove the existence of correlations between linguistic structure and nonlinguistic behavior. It would be fruitless to go about asking people of various cultures their opinions as to whether the language they spoke had determined the manner in which they thought, had dictated their view of the world. Nobody would be able to answer such a question, for a people's language is so completely embedded in their consciousness that they would be unable to conceive of any other way of interpreting the world.

Despite the near impossibility of proving or disproving Whorf's theory, it will not go away but keeps coming back, intriguing each succeeding generation of linguists. It is certainly one of the most fascinating theories created by the modern mind. It is comparable in some ways to Einstein's theory of relativity. Just as Einstein said that how people saw the phenomena of the universe was relative to their point of observation, so Whorf said that a people's world view was relative to the language they spoke.

And demonstrations of Whorf's ideas are not entirely lacking. They come mainly from studies of color—one of the very few aspects of reality that can be specified by objective scientific methods and also is rather precisely specified by people's naming of colors. In this instance it is possible to compare one person's language, expressing that person's view of the world, with another's language for exactly the same characteristic of the world. The comparison can thus reveal different views that are linked to different descriptions of the same reality. English-speakers view purple as a single relatively uniform color; only if pressed and then only with difficulty will they make any attempt to divide it into such shades as lavender and mauve. But no English-speaker would lump orange with purple; to the users of English, those colors are completely separate, for no single word includes both of them. If other languages made different distinctions in the naming of color—if lavender and mauve were always separate, never encompassed by a word for purple, or if orange and purple were not distinguished but were called by a name that covered both—then it would seem that the users of those languages interpreted those colors differently.

Such differences in color-naming, it turns out, are fairly widespread. Linguist H. A. Gleason compared the color spectrum as described by English-speaking persons to the way it was labeled by speakers of Bassa, a language spoken in Liberia, and by speakers of Shona, spoken in Rhodesia. English-speaking people, when seeing sunlight refracted through a prism, identify by name at least six colors—purple, blue, green, yellow, orange, and red. The speakers of Shona, however, have only three names for the colors of the spectrum. They group orange, red, and purple under one name. They also lump blue and green-blue under one of their other color terms and use their third word to identify yellow and the yellower hues of green. The speakers of Bassa are similarly restricted by a lack of handy terms for color, for they have only two words for the hues of the spectrum.

Gleason's observations prompted psychologists to perform an experiment that also showed the influence words can have on the way colors are handled intellectually and remembered. It was an ingenious and complex experiment with many checks and double checks of the results, but in essence it boiled down to something like this: English-speaking subjects were shown a series of color samples—rather like the little "chips" provided by a paint store to help customers decide what color to paint the living room. The subjects were then asked to pick out the colors they had seen from a far larger array of colors. It turned out that they could more accurately pick out the right colors from the larger selection when the color involved had a handy, ordinary name like "green." The subjects had difficulty with the ambiguous, in-between colors such as off-purples and misty blues. In other words, a person can remember a color better if that person's language offers a handy label for it, but has trouble when the language does not offer such a familiar term. Again the human ability to differentiate reality seemed to be affected by the resources offered by language.

Richness of linguistic resource undoubtedly helps people to cope with subtle gradations in the things they deal with every day. The Hanunóo people of the Philippine Islands have different names for ninety-two varieties of rice. They can easily distinguish differences in rice that would be all but invisible to English-speaking people, who lump all such grains under the single word *rice*. Of course, English-speakers can make distinctions by resorting to adjectives and perhaps differentiate long-grain, brown rice from small-grain, yellow rice, but surely no European or American would, lacking the terms, have a sufficiently practiced eye to distinguish ninety-two varieties of rice. Language is essentially a code that people use both to think and to communicate. As psychologist Roger Brown sums up the rice question: "Among the Hanunóo, who have names for ninety-two varieties of rice, any one of those varieties is highly codable in the array of ninety-one other varieties. The Hanunóo have a word for it and so can transmit it efficiently and presumably can recognize it easily. Among speakers of English one kind of rice among ninety-one other kinds would have very low codability."

Brown goes on to suppose that the Hanunóo set down in New York would be baffled by the reality around them partly because they would then be the ones lacking the needed words. "If the Hanunóo were to visit the annual Automobile Show in New York City, they would find it difficult to encode distinctively any particular automobile in that array. But an American having such lexical resources as *Chevrolet, Ford, Plymouth, Buick, Corvette, hard-top, convertible, four-door, station wagon,* and the like could easily encode ninety-two varieties."

The very existence of so many different languages, each linked to a distinctive culture, is itself support of a sort for Whorf's hypothesis. At least since the time of the Tower of Babel, no single tongue has been shared by all the people of the world. Many attempts have been made to invent an international language, one so simply structured and easy to learn it would be used by everyone around the globe as a handy adjunct to their native speech. Yet even the most successful of these world languages, Esperanto, has found but limited acceptance.

There are international languages, however, to serve international cultures. The intellectual disciplines of music, dance, and mathematics might be considered specialized cultures; each is shared by people around the world, and each has an international language, used as naturally in Peking as in Paris. English is a world language in certain activities that straddle national boundaries, such as international air travel; it serves for communications between international flights and the ground in every country—a Lufthansa pilot approaching Athens talks with the airport control tower neither in German nor in Greek but in English.

The trouble with most attempts to lend credence to the Sapir-Whorf hypothesis is that, while they indicate connections between culture and language, they do not really prove that a language shaped its users' view of the world. Just because the speakers of Shona have only three main distinctions of color does not mean that their "world view" is all that different from that of the English-speaker who has more convenient color terms. Shona speakers obviously see all the colors in the rainbow that English-speakers see. Their eyes are physiologically the same. Their comparative poverty of words for those colors merely means that it is harder for them to talk about color. Their "code" is not so handy; the colors' codability is lower.

Critics also point out that Whorf may have mistaken what are called dead metaphors for real differences in the Hopi language. All languages are loaded with dead metaphors—figures of speech that have lost all figurative value and are now just familiar words. The word "goodbye" is a dead metaphor. Once it meant "God be with you," but in its contracted form it conjures up no thought or picture of God. If a Whorfian linguist who was a native speaker of Hopi turned the tables and analyzed English he might conclude that English-speakers were perpetually thinking of religion since this everyday word incorporates a reference to God—a ridiculous misreading of a term that has lost all of its original religious significance. In like fashion, perhaps Whorf was reading too much into the Hopi lexicon and grammar, seeing significances where there were none.

The argument about how far Whorf's ideas can be stretched has gone on for several decades and promises to go on for several more. Most psychologists believe that all people see pretty much the same reality; their languages merely have different words and structures to approximate in various idiosyncratic ways a picture of that reality. And yet the experts accept what might be called modified Whorfism—a belief in the power of language to affect, if not to direct, the perception of reality. If a language is rich in terms for certain things or ideas—possesses extensive codability for them—then the people speaking that language can conceive of, and talk about, those things or ideas more conveniently. If different languages do not give their speakers entirely different world views, they certainly influence thinking to some degree.

Even within the Indo-European family of languages, some tongues have words for concepts that other tongues lack. German is especially rich in philosophical terms that have no exact counterparts in English, French, Italian—or any known language. One is *Weltschmerz*, which combines in itself meanings that it takes three English phrases to adequately convey—"weariness of life," "pessimistic outlook," and "romantic discontent." Another German word that has no direct translation is *Weltanschauung*. To approximate its meaning in English requires a number of different terms—"philosophy of life," "world outlook," "ideology"—for all of these elements are included in the German word. *Weltanschauung* is untranslatable into any single English term. It represents an idea for which only German has a word. Possessing the convenient term, German writers can develop this idea more easily than the users of other languages, and thus explore its ramifications further.

Even when a word from one language may seem to be easily translatable into another, it often is not really equivalent. The French term *distingué* would appear to translate easily enough into the English *distinguished*. But the French use their word in ways that no English-speaker would ever employ for *distinguished*. A Frenchman might reprimand his son by saying that his impolite behavior was not *distingué* or he might tell his wife that a scarf she has worn out to dinner is charmingly *distingué*. The word does not mean "distinguished" as English-speakers employ the term, but something more like "suitable," or "appropriate," or "in keeping with polite standards." It is simply not the same word in the two languages no matter how similar the spelling. It represents a different idea, connoting a subtle difference in mental style.

In some cases the existence of a word leads users of it down tortured logical paths toward dead ends. The common word *nothing* is one example. Since there is a word for the concept, points out philosopher George Pitcher, it tempts people to think that "nothing" is a real entity, that somehow it exists, a palpable realm of not-being. It has in fact led a number of philosophers, including the twentieth-century French thinker Jean-Paul Sartre, to spend a great deal of effort speculating about the nature of "nothing." The difficulty of this philosophic dilemma is indicated by a typical Sartre sentence on the subject: "The Being by which Nothingness arrives in the world must nihilate. Nothingness in its Being, and even so it still runs the risk of establishing Nothingness as a transcendent in the very heart of immanence unless it nihilates Nothingness in its being in connection with its own being." Sartre could hardly have gotten himself tangled up in such agonized prose had French lacked a noun for *le neant*, nothing, and the value to human welfare of his attempt to explain is open to question.

The power of language to influence the world can be seen not only in comparisons of one tongue to another, but also within a single language. The way in which people use their native tongue—choosing one term over another to express the same idea or action, varying structures or phrases for different situations—has a strong effect on their attitudes toward those situations. Distasteful ideas can be made to seem acceptable or even desirable by careful choices of words, and language can make actions or beliefs that might otherwise be considered correct appear to be obsolescent or naive. Value judgments of many kinds can be attached to seemingly simple statements. Shakespeare may have believed that "a rose by any other name would smell as sweet," but he was wrong, as other theatrical promoters have proved repeatedly. A young English vaudevillian known as Archibald Leach was a minor comedian until he was given the more romantic name of Cary Grant. The new name did not make him a star, but it did create an atmosphere in which he could demonstrate his talent, suggesting the type of character he came to exemplify.

If the power of a stage name to characterize personality seems of relatively minor consequence in human affairs, consider the effect of a different sort of appellation: "boy." It was—and sometimes still is—the form of address employed by whites in the American South in speaking to black males of any age. This word, many authorities believe, served as an instrument of subjugation. It implied that the black was not a man but a child, someone not mature enough to be entrusted with responsibility for himself, let alone authority over others. His inferior position was thus made to seem natural and justified, and it could be enforced without compunction.

Characterizing people by tagging them with a word label is a world-wide practice. Many peoples use a single word to designate both themselves and the human race. "The Carib Indians, for example, have stated with no equivocation, 'We alone are people,' " reported anthropologist Jack Conrad. "Similarly, the ancient Egyptians used the word *romet* (men) only among themselves and in no case for strangers. The Lapps of Scandinavia reserve the term 'human being' for those of their own kind, while the Cherokee Indians call themselves *Ani-Yun-wiya*, which means 'principal people.' The Kiowa Indians of the Southwest are willing to accept other peoples as human, but the very name, *Kiowa*, meaning 'real people,' shows their true feeling." The effect of reserving a term indicating "human" to one group is far-reaching. It alters the perception of anyone from outside that group. He is not called "human," and need not be treated as human.

Like an animal, he can be entrapped, beaten, or even killed with more or less impunity. This use of a word to demote whole groups from the human class is often a wartime tactic—the enemy is referred to by a pejorative name to justify killing him.

While language can be twisted to make ordinarily good things seem bad, it can also be twisted in the opposite direction to make bad things seem good or run-of-the-mill things better than they really are. The technique depends on the employment of euphemisms, a term derived from the Greek for "words of good omen." A euphemism is roundabout language that is intended to conceal something embarrassing or unpleasant. Some classes of euphemism—little evasions that people use every day—are inoffensive enough. It is when such cloudy doubletalk invades the vital areas of politics and foreign affairs that it becomes perilous.

A large and commonly used—and relatively harmless—class of euphemism has to do with bodily functions. Many people shy away from frank talk about excretion or sex; in fact, many of the old, vivid terms—the four-letter words—are socially taboo. So people for centuries have skirted the edge of such matters, inventing a rich vocabulary of substitute terms. Americans offered turkey on Thanksgiving commonly say "white meat" or "dark meat" to announce their preference. These terms date back to the nineteenth century when it was considered indelicate to say "breast" or "leg." *Toilet,* itself a euphemism coined from the French *toilette* ("making oneself presentable to the outside world"), long ago became tainted and too graphic for the prudish. The list of euphemistic substitutes is almost endless, ranging from the commonplace *washroom, bathroom,* and *restroom* (whoever rests in a restroom?) to *john, head,* and *Chic Sale* in the United States, and in England the *loo. Loo* may be derived from a mistaken English pronunciation of the French *l'eau,* water. Or it may be a euphemism derived from a euphemism. The French, with Gallic delicacy, once commonly put the number 100 on bathroom doors in hotels. It is easy to see how an English person might have mistaken the number for the word *loo.* Meanwhile, ladies in restaurants have adopted "I'm going to powder my nose" or, in England, where it once cost a penny to use public toilets, "I'm going to spend a penny."

Another generally harmless use of euphemistic language is the practice, especially notable in the United States, of giving prestigious names to more-or-less ordinary trades. As H. L. Mencken pointed out in *The American Language,* his masterly examination of English as spoken in the United States, ratcatchers are fond of calling themselves "exterminating engineers" and hairdressers have long since showed a preference for "beautician." The *-ician* ending, in fact, has proved very popular, doubtless because it echoes "physician" and thus sounds both professional and scientific. In the late nineteenth century undertakers had already begun to call themselves "funeral directors," but starting in 1916 ennobled themselves even further by battening on the newer euphemistic coinage, "mortician." Meanwhile a tree trimmer became a "tree surgeon" (that love of medicine again) and a press agent became a "publicist" or, even more grandly, a "public relations counsel."

Americans (and the English, too) not only chose high-sounding euphemisms for their professions but also gave new and gaudy names to their places of business. Thus pawn shops became "loan offices," saloons became "cocktail rooms," pool halls became "billiard parlors," and barber shops "hair-styling salons."

Purists might say that such shading or blunting of the stark truth leads to moral decay, but it is difficult to see why anybody should be the worse for allowing women to excuse themselves by pleading that they must powder their noses. There are euphemisms, however, that are clearly anything but harmless. These are evasive, beclouding phraseologies that hide truths people must clearly perceive if they are to govern themselves intelligently and keep a check on those in positions of power. Slick phrases, slippery evasions—words deliberately designed to hide unpleasant truth rather than reveal it—can so becloud political processes and so easily hide mistaken policies that the entire health of a nation is imperiled.

The classic treatise on the political misuse of language in modern times is the 1946 essay "Politics and the English Language" by the British writer George Orwell. "In our time, political speech and writing are largely the defence of the indefencible," Orwell said. "Thus political language has to consist largely of euphemism, question-begging and sheer cloudy vagueness." He concluded, "Such phraseology is needed if one wants to name things without calling up mental pictures of them. . . . When there is a gap between one's real and one's declared aims, one turns as it were instinctively to long words and exhausted idioms, like a cuttlefish squirting out ink."

Orwell supplied numerous examples to buttress his charges. "Defenceless villages are bombarded from the air, the inhabitants driven out into the country-side, the cattle machine-gunned, the huts set on fire with incendiary bullets: this is called *pacification*." He went on to observe that in Stalin's Russia people were "imprisoned for years without trial or shot in the back of the neck or sent to die of scurvy in Arctic lumber camps: this is called *elimination of unreliable elements.*"

Orwell, who died at the age of forty-six in 1950, did not live to collect even more deplorable distortions of language. The French clothed their brutal war in Algeria with a veil of euphemism; the North Koreans accused the South Koreans of "aggression" when the North invaded the South. The United States invented a whole lexicon of gobbledygook to disguise the horror of the war in Vietnam: "protective reaction strike" (the bombing of a Vietnamese village); "surgical bombing" (the same as protective reaction strike); "free-fire zone" (an area in which troops could shoot anything that moved, including helpless villagers); "new life hamlet" (a refugee camp for survivors of a surgical bombing).

Perhaps the most appalling use of this type of euphemism was the word employed by the Nazis for their program to exterminate all of Europe's Jews. The word is *Endlösung*, which means final solution. Behind that verbal façade the Nazis gassed, burned, shot, or worked to death some six million Jews from Germany, France, Poland, and other conquered parts of Europe. Hitler and

Gestapo chief Himmler often employed the euphemism among themselves, and it was always used in official records—but not necessarily to preserve secrecy for purposes of state security. Apparently the euphemism shielded the Nazis from themselves. Openly brutal and murderous as they were, they could not face up to the horrible reality of what they were doing, and they had to hide it in innocuous language.

Such distortion of language can do more than disguise truth. It can turn truth around, so that the idea conveyed is the opposite of actuality. After the USSR savagely crushed the Hungarian rebellion in 1956 the Soviet aggression was made to seem, in the twisted language used by other Communist dictatorships, an expression of friendship. The Peking radio commented after the rebellion was put down: "The Hungarian people can see that Soviet policy toward the people's democracies is truly one of equality, friendship, and mutual assistance, not of conquest, aggression, and plunder."

The possibility that such topsy-turvy language might ultimately make the world topsy-turvy—an ironic demonstration of the fundamental truth of Benjamin Lee Whorf's insights—was raised in a dramatic way by George Orwell. His novel *1984*, a chilling and convincing description of life in a totalitarian society, shows how language might destroy reality. In the imaginary nation of Oceania the official language is Newspeak, which is intended to facilitate "doublethink," the ability to accept simultaneously ideas contradicting each other. The Oceania state apparatus includes a Ministry of Truth, its headquarters building emblazoned with three slogans: "WAR IS PEACE"; "FREEDOM IS SLAVERY"; "IGNORANCE IS STRENGTH." There are also other ministries, Orwell explained: "The Ministry of Peace, which concerned itself with war; the Ministry of Love, which maintained law and order." Anyone who would use language this way, Orwell made clear, denies the meaning of his or her words. He or she has lost touch with reality and substituted for it an emptiness concealed in sounds that once had meaning.

There is another threat to language besides the intentional twisting of words by demagogues and others who would control people's thoughts. It is less obvious, but a danger nevertheless: simple imprecision, slovenliness, mindlessness in the use of the language. It seems a small matter that English-speakers increasingly confuse *uninterested* with *disinterested*, for example. But these words do not mean the same thing. *Disinterested* means impartial, not taking sides. *Uninterested* means lacking in interest, bored. A judge should be *disinterested* but never *uninterested*. Many such changes result from the inevitable evolution of language as it changes over the years, but the change can be a loss. The slow erosion of distinctions, visible in much writing, audible in many conversations, makes language imprecise and thus clumsy and ineffective as communication.

Among the symptoms of such erosion are stock phrases that people mindlessly repeat, substituting noise for thought. Everyone has heard speechmakers use such clichés as "having regard to," "play into the hands of," "in the interest of," "no axe to grind." Although this brief list is drawn from Orwell's essay of

1946 these exhausted clichés are still heard. Such verbal dead limbs do not distort thought but rather tend to obliterate it in a cloud of meaninglessness. "The slovenliness of our language makes it easier for us to have foolish thoughts," wrote Orwell. And ultimately, as has been pointed out by commentator Edwin Newman in his book *Strictly Speaking,* "Those for whom words have lost their value are likely to find that ideas have also lost their value."

Review Questions

1. According to Thomson, what is the Sapir-Whorf hypothesis? Give some examples.

2. According to Whorf, how can grammar affect people's perceptions? Give examples.

3. The Sapir-Whorf hypothesis has been tested in several ways. What are some of the tests of the hypothesis described by Thomson, and how have these modified the theory?

4. What are some of the ways in which language affects or modifies perception in modern America? Can you add examples from your own experience to those presented by Thomson?

Introduction and Review Questions reprinted from *Conformity and Conflict: Readings in Cultural Anthropology*, 12/e, Ed. James Spradley and David W. McCurdy, (2006), by permission of Allyn and Bacon.

5

Baseball Magic

George Gmelch

Americans pride themselves on their scientific approach to life and problem solving. But as George Gmelch demonstrates in this article, U.S. baseball players, much like people in many parts of the world, also turn to supernatural forces to ensure success. Following the pioneering analysis of Trobriand magic by Bronislaw Malinowski, Gmelch shows that, like Trobriand Islanders, baseball players use magic, including ritual, taboos, and fetishes, to manage the anxiety generated by unpredictable events that challenge human control.

On each pitching day for the first three months of a winning season, Dennis Grossini, a pitcher on a Detroit Tiger farm team, arose from bed at exactly 10:00 A.M. At 1:00 P.M. he went to the nearest restaurant for two glasses of iced tea and a tuna fish sandwich. When he got to the ballpark at 3:00 P.M., he put on the sweatshirt and jock he wore during his last winning game; one hour before the game he chewed a wad of Beech-Nut chewing tobacco. After each pitch during the game he touched the letters on his uniform and straightened his cap

Reprinted from *Conformity and Conflict: Readings in Cultural Anthropology,* Twelfth Edition, edited by James Spradley and David W. McCurdy (2006), Allyn & Bacon. Copyright © 2006 by George Gmelch.

after each ball. Before the start of each inning he replaced the pitcher's rosin bag next to the spot where it was the inning before. And after every inning in which he gave up a run, he washed his hands.

When I asked which part of his ritual was most important, he said, "You can't really tell what's most important so it all becomes important. I'd be afraid to change anything. As long as I'm winning, I do everything the same."

Trobriand Islanders, according to anthropologist Bronislaw Malinowski, felt the same way about their fishing magic. Trobrianders fished in two different settings: in the *inner lagoon* where fish were plentiful and there was little danger, and on the *open sea* where fishing was dangerous and yields varied widely. Malinowski found that magic was not used in lagoon fishing, where men could rely solely on their knowledge and skill. But when fishing on the open sea, Trobrianders used a great deal of magical ritual to ensure safety and increase their catch.

Baseball, America's national pastime, is an arena in which players behave remarkably like Malinowski's Trobriand fishermen. To professional ballplayers, baseball is more than a game, it is an occupation. Because their livelihoods depend on how well they perform, many use magic in an attempt to control the chance that is built into baseball. There are three essential activities of the game: pitching, hitting, and fielding. In the first two, chance can play a surprisingly important role. The pitcher is the player least able to control the outcome of his efforts. He may feel great and have good stuff warming up in the bullpen and then get in the game and get clobbered. He may make a bad pitch and see the batter miss it for a strike or see it hit hard but right into the hands of a fielder for an out. Conversely, his best pitch may be blooped for a base hit. He may limit the opposing team to just a few hits yet lose the game, and he may give up many hits and win. And the good and bad luck don't always average out over the course of a season. For instance, this past season Jeriome Robertson gave up 1.4 more runs per game than his teammate Tim Redding but had a better win–loss record. Robertson went 15–9, while Redding was only 10–14. Both pitched for the same team—the Houston Astros—which meant they had the same fielders behind them. Regardless of how well a pitcher performs, the outcome of the game also depends upon the proficiency of his teammates, the ineptitude of the opposition, and luck.

Hitting, which many observers call the single most difficult task in the world of sports, is also full of uncertainty. Unless it's a home run, no matter how hard the batter hits the ball, fate determines whether it will go into a waiting glove or find a gap between the fielders. The uncertainty is compounded by the low success rate of hitting: the average hitter gets only one hit in every four trips to the plate, while the very best hitters average only one hit in every three trips. Fielding, which we will return to later, is the one part of baseball where chance does not play much of a role.

How does the risk and uncertainty in pitching and hitting affect players? How do they try to control the outcomes of their performance? These are questions that I first became interested in many years ago both as a ballplayer and as an anthropology student. I had devoted much of my youth to baseball, and played professionally as a first baseman in the Detroit Tiger organization in the 1960s. It was shortly after the end of one baseball season that I took an anthropology course called "Magic, Religion, and Witchcraft." As I listened to my professor describe the magical rituals of the Trobriand Islanders, it occurred to me that what these so-called "primitive" people did wasn't all that different from what my teammates and I did for luck and confidence at the ballpark.

Routines and Rituals

The most common way players attempt to reduce chance and their feelings of uncertainty is to develop a daily routine—a course of action which is regularly followed. Talking about the routines of ballplayers, Pittsburgh Pirates' coach Rich Donnelly said:

> They're like trained animals. They come out here [ballpark] and everything has to be the same, they don't like anything that knocks them off their routine. Just look at the dugout and you'll see every guy sitting in the same spot every night. It's amazing, everybody in the same spot. And don't you dare take someone's seat. If a guy comes up from the minors and sits here, they'll say, "Hey, Jim sits here, find another seat." You watch the pitcher warm up and he'll do the same thing every time. . . . You got a routine and you adhere to it and you don't want anybody knocking you off it.

Routines are comforting; they bring order into a world in which players have little control. And sometimes practical elements in routines produce tangible benefits, such as helping the player concentrate. But some of what players do goes beyond mere routine. These actions become what anthropologists define as *ritual*—prescribed behaviors in which there is no empirical connection between the means (e.g., tapping home plate three times) and the desired end (e.g., getting a base hit). Because there is no real connection between the two, rituals are not rational. Sometimes they are quite irrational. Similar to rituals are the nonrational beliefs that form the basis of taboos and fetishes, which players also use to bring luck to their side. But first let's take a close look at rituals.

Baseball rituals are infinitely varied. Most are personal, performed by individuals rather than by a team or group. Most are done in an unemotional manner, in much the same way players apply pine tar to their bats to improve the grip or dab eye black on their upper cheeks to reduce the sun's glare. A ballplayer may ritualize any activity that he considers important or somehow linked to good performance. Recall the variety of things that Dennis Grossini does, from specific times for waking and eating to foods and dress. Jason Bere of the White Sox listens to the same song on his Walkman before he pitches. Atlanta Brave Denny Neagle goes to a movie on days he is scheduled to start. Baltimore Oriole Glenn Davis used to chew the same gum every day during hitting streaks, saving it under his cap. Astros Infielder Julio Gotay always played with a cheese sandwich in his back pocket (he had a big appetite, so there might also have been a measure of practicality here). Wade Boggs of the Red Sox ate chicken before every game during his career, and that was just one of many elements in his pre- and postgame routine, which also included leaving his house for the ballpark at precisely the same time each day (1:47 for a 7:05 game).

Many hitters go through a series of preparatory rituals before stepping into the batter's box. These include tugging on their caps, touching their uniform letters or medallions, crossing themselves, and swinging, tapping, or bouncing the bat on the plate a prescribed number of times. Consider Cubs shortstop Nomar Garciaparra. After each pitch he steps out of the batters box, kicks the dirt with each toe, adjusts his right batting glove, adjusts his left batting glove, and touches his helmet before getting back into the box. Mike Hargrove, former Cleveland Indian first baseman, had so many time-consuming elements in his batting ritual that he was nicknamed "the human rain delay." Both players believe their batting rituals helped them regain their concentration after each pitch. But others wondered if the two had become prisoners of their superstitions. Another ritual associated with hitting is tagging a base when leaving and returning to the dugout between innings. Some players don't "feel right" unless they tag a specific base on each trip between dugout and field. One of my teammates added some complexity to his ritual by tagging third base on his way to the dugout only after the third, sixth, and ninth innings.

Players who have too many or particularly bizarre rituals risk being labeled as flakes, and not just by teammates but by fans and the media as well. For example, Mets pitcher Turk Wendell's eccentric rituals, which include wearing a necklace of teeth from animals he has killed, made him a cover story subject in the *New York Times Sunday Magazine*.

Baseball fans observe a lot of this ritual behavior, such as pitchers smoothing the dirt on the mound before each new batter, never realizing its importance to the player. The one ritual many fans do recognize, largely because it's a favorite of TV cameramen, is the "rally cap"—players in the dugout folding their caps and wearing them bill up in hopes of sparking a rally.

Most rituals grow out of exceptionally good performances. When a player does well, he seldom attributes his success to skill alone; he knows that his skills don't change much from day to day. So, then, what was different about today that can explain his three hits? He may attribute his success, in part, to an object, a food he ate, not having shaved, a new shirt he bought that day, or just about any behavior out of the ordinary. By repeating those behaviors, the player seeks to gain control over his performance, to bring more good luck. Outfielder John White explained how one of his rituals started:

> I was jogging out to centerfield after the national anthem when I picked up a scrap of paper. I got some good hits that night and I guess I decided that the paper had something to do with it. The next night I picked up a gum wrapper and had another good night at the plate. . . . I've been picking up paper every night since.

When outfielder Ron Wright played for the Calgary Cannons he shaved his arms once a week. It all began two years before when after an injury he shaved his arm so it could be taped, and then hit three homers. Now he not only has one of the smoothest swings in the minor leagues, but two of the smoothest forearms. Wade Boggs' routine of eating chicken before every game began when he was a rookie in 1982 and noticed a correlation between multiple-hit games and poultry plates (his wife has 40 chicken recipes). One of Montreal Expo farmhand Mike Saccocio's rituals also concerned food: "I got three hits one night after eating at Long John Silver's. After that when we'd pull into town, my first question would be, "Do you have a Long John Silver's?" Unlike Boggs, Saccocio abandoned his ritual and looked for a new one when he stopped hitting well.

When in a slump, most players make a deliberate effort to change their routines and rituals in an attempt to shake off their bad luck. One player tried taking different routes to the ballpark, another tried sitting in a different place in the dugout, another shaved his head, and several reported changing what they ate before the game. Years ago, some of my teammates rubbed their hands along the handles of the bats protruding from the bat bin in hopes of picking up some power or luck from the bats of others. I had one manager who would rattle the bat bin when the team was not hitting well, as if the bats were in a stupor and could be aroused by a good shaking.

Taboo

Taboos (the word comes from a Polynesian term meaning prohibition) are the opposite of rituals. These are things you shouldn't do. Breaking a taboo, players believe, leads to undesirable consequences or bad luck. Most players observe at least a few taboos, such as never stepping on the white foul lines. A few, like Nomar Garciaparra, leap over the entire basepath. One teammate of mine would never watch a movie on a game day, despite the fact that we played nearly every day from April to September. Another teammate refused to read anything before a game because he believed it weakened his batting eye.

Many taboos take place off the field, out of public view. On the day a pitcher is scheduled to start, he is likely to avoid activities he believes will sap his strength and detract from his effectiveness. Some pitchers avoid eating certain foods, others will not shave on the day of a game, refusing to shave again as long as they are winning. Early in one season Oakland's Dave Stewart had six consecutive victories and a beard by the time he lost.

Taboos usually grow out of exceptionally poor performances, which players, in search of a reason, attribute to a particular behavior. During my first season of pro ball I ate pancakes before a game in which I struck out three times. A few weeks later I had another terrible game, again after eating pancakes. The result was a pancake taboo: I never again ate pancakes during the season. Pitcher Jason Bere has a taboo that makes more sense in dietary terms: after eating a meatball sandwich and not pitching well, he swore off them for the rest of the season.

While most taboos are idiosyncratic, there are a few that all ballplayers hold and that do not develop out of individual experience or misfortune. These form part of the culture of baseball, and are sometimes learned as early as Little League. Mentioning a no-hitter while one is in progress is a well-known example.

Fetishes

Fetishes are charms, material objects believed to embody supernatural power that can aid or protect the owner. Good-luck charms are standard equipment for some ballplayers. These include a wide assortment of objects from coins, chains, and crucifixes to a favorite baseball hat. The fetishized object may be a new possession or something a player found that coincided with the start of a streak and which he holds responsible for his good fortune. While playing in the Pacific Coast League, Alan Foster forgot his baseball shoes on a road trip and borrowed a pair from a teammate. That night he pitched a no-hitter, which he attributed to the shoes. Afterwards he bought them from his teammate and they became a fetish. Expo farmhand Mark LaRosa's rock has a different origin and use:

> I found it on the field in Elmira after I had gotten bombed. It's unusual, perfectly round, and it caught my attention. I keep it to remind me of how important it is to concentrate. When I am going well I look at the rock and remember to keep my focus. The rock reminds me of what can happen when I lose my concentration.

For one season Marge Schott, former owner of the Cincinnati Reds, insisted that her field manager rub her St. Bernard "Schotzie" for good luck before each game. When the Reds were on the road, Schott would sometimes send a bag of the dog's hair to the field manager's hotel room. Religious medallions, which many Latino players wear around their necks and sometimes touch before going to the plate or mound, are also fetishes, though tied to their Roman Catholicism. Also relating to their religion, some players make the sign of the cross or bless themselves before every at bat (a few like Pudge Rodriguez do so before every pitch), and a few point to the heavens after hitting a home run.

Some players regard certain uniform numbers as lucky. When Ricky Henderson came to the Blue Jays in 1993, he paid teammate Turner Ward $25,000 for the right to wear number 24. Don Sutton got off cheaper. When he joined the Dodgers he convinced teammate Bruce Boche to give up number 20 in exchange for a new set of golf clubs. Oddly enough, there is no consensus about the effect of wearing number 13. Some players shun it, while a few request it. When Jason Giambi arrived with the Oakland A's his favorite number 7 was already taken, so he settled for 16 (the two numbers add up to 7). When he signed with the Yankees, number 7 (Mickey Mantle's old number) was retired and 16 was taken, so he settled for 25 (again, the numbers add up to 7).

Number preferences emerge in different ways. A young player may request the number of a former star, sometimes hoping that it will bring him the same success. Or he may request a number he associates with good luck. Colorado

Rockies' Larry Walker's fixation with the number 3 has become well known to baseball fans. Besides wearing 33, he takes three practice swings before stepping into the box, he showers from the third nozzle, sets his alarm for three minutes past the hour and he was married on November 3 at 3:33 P.M.[1] Fans in ballparks all across America rise from their seats for the seventh-inning stretch before the home club comes to bat because the number 7 is lucky, although the specific origin of this tradition has been lost.

Clothing, both the choice and the order in which it is put on, combine elements of both ritual and fetish. Some players put on the part of their uniform in a particular order. Expos farmhand Jim Austin always puts on his left sleeve, left pants leg, and left shoe before the right. Most players, however, single out one or two lucky articles or quirks of dress for ritual elaboration. After hitting two home runs in a game, for example, ex-Giant infielder Jim Davenport discovered that he had missed a buttonhole while dressing for the game. For the remainder of his career he left the same button undone. Phillies' Len Dykstra would discard his batting gloves if he failed to get a hit in a single at-bat. In a hitless game, he might go through four pair of gloves. For outfielder Brian Hunter the focus is shoes: "I have a pair of high tops and a pair of low tops. Whichever shoes don't get a hit that game, I switch to the other pair." At the time of our interview, he was struggling at the plate and switching shoes almost every day. For Birmingham Baron pitcher Bo Kennedy the arrangement of the different pairs of baseball shoes in his locker is critical:

> I tell the clubbies [clubhouse boys] when you hang stuff in my locker don't touch my shoes. If you bump them move them back. I want the Ponys in front, the turfs to the right, and I want them nice and neat with each pair touching each other. . . . Everyone on the team knows not to mess with my shoes when I pitch.

During hitting or winning streaks players may wear the same clothes day after day. Once I changed sweatshirts midway through the game for seven consecutive nights to keep a hitting streak going. Clothing rituals, however, can become impractical. Catcher Matt Allen was wearing a long sleeve turtle neck shirt on a cool evening in the New York-Penn League when he had a three-hit game. "I kept wearing the shirt and had a good week," he explained. "Then the weather got hot as hell, 85 degrees and muggy, but I would not take that shirt off. I wore it for another ten days—catching—and people thought I was crazy." Former Phillies, Expos, Twins, and Angels manager Gene Mauch never washed his underwear or uniform after a win. Perhaps taking a ritual to the extreme, Leo Durocher, managing the Brooklyn Dodgers to a pennant in 1941, spent three and a half weeks in the same gray slacks, blue coat, and knitted blue tie. Losing can produce the opposite effect, such as the Oakland A's players who went out and bought new street clothes in an attempt to break a 14-game losing streak.

---

[1] Lee Allen, "The Superstitions of Baseball Players," *New York Folklore Quarterly* 20, no. 20 (1964): 98–109.

Baseball's superstitions, like most everything else, change over time. Many of the rituals and beliefs of early baseball are no longer observed. In the 1920s–30s sportswriters reported that a player who tripped en route to the field would often retrace his steps and carefully walk over the stumbling block for "insurance." A century ago players spent time on and off the field intently looking for items that would bring them luck. To find a hairpin on the street, for example, assured a batter of hitting safely in that day's game. A few managers were known to strategically place a hairpin on the ground where a slumping player would be sure to find it. Today few women wear hairpins—a good reason the belief has died out. In the same era, Philadelphia Athletics manager Connie Mack hoped to ward off bad luck by employing a hunchback as a mascot. Hall of Famer Ty Cobb took on a young black boy as a good luck charm, even taking him on the road during the 1908 season. It was a not uncommon then for players to rub the head of a black child for good luck.

To catch sight of a white horse or a wagon-load of barrels were also good omens. In 1904 the manager of the New York Giants, John McGraw, hired a driver with a team of white horses to drive past the Polo Grounds around the time his players were arriving at the ballpark. He knew that if his players saw white horses, they would have more confidence and that could only help them during the game. Belief in the power of white horses survived in a few backwaters until the 1960s. A gray-haired manager of a team I played for in Drummondville, Quebec, would drive around the countryside before important games and during the playoffs looking for a white horse. When he was successful, he would announce it to everyone in the clubhouse.

One belief that appears to have died out recently is a taboo about crossed bats. Some of my Latino teammates in the 1960s took it seriously. I can still recall one Dominican player becoming agitated when another player tossed a bat from the batting cage and it landed on top of his bat. He believed that the top bat might steal hits from the lower one. In his view, bats contained a finite number of hits. It was once commonly believed that when the hits in a bat were used up no amount of good hitting would produce any more. Hall of Famer Honus Wagner believed each bat contained only 100 hits. Regardless of the quality of the bat, he would discard it after its 100th hit. This belief would have little relevance today, in the era of light bats with thin handles—so thin that the typical modern bat is lucky to survive a dozen hits without being broken. Other superstitions about bats do survive, however. Position players on the Class A Asheville Tourists would not let pitchers touch or swing their bats, not even to warm up. Poor-hitting players, as most pitchers are, were said to pollute or weaken the bats.

Uncertainty and Magic

The best evidence that players turn to rituals, taboos, and fetishes to control chance and uncertainty is found in their uneven application. They are associated mainly with pitching and hitting—the activities with the highest degree of chance—and not fielding. I met only one player who had any ritual in connection with fielding, and he was an error-prone shortstop. Unlike hitting and pitching, a fielder has almost complete control over the outcome of his performance. Once a ball has been hit in his direction, no one can intervene and ruin his chances of catching it for an out (except in the unlikely event of two fielders colliding). Compared with the pitcher or the hitter, the fielder has little to worry about. He knows that in better than 9.7 times out of 10 he will execute his task flawlessly. With odds like that there is little need for ritual.

Clearly, the rituals of American ballplayers are not unlike those of the Trobriand Islanders studied by Malinowski many years ago.[2] In professional baseball, fielding is the equivalent of the inner lagoon while hitting and pitching are like the open sea.

While Malinowski helps us understand how ballplayers respond to chance and uncertainty, behavioral psychologist B. F. Skinner sheds light on why personal rituals get established in the first place.[3] With a few grains of seed Skinner could get pigeons to do anything he wanted. He merely waited for the desired behavior (e.g., pecking) and then rewarded it with some food. Skinner then decided to see what would happen if pigeons were rewarded with food pellets regularly, every fifteen seconds, regardless of what they did. He found that the birds associate the arrival of the food with a particular action, such as tucking their head under a wing or walking in clockwise circles. About ten seconds after the arrival of the last pellet, a bird would begin doing whatever it associated with getting the food and keep doing it until the next pellet arrived. In short, the pigeons behaved as if their actions made the food appear. They learned to associate particular behaviors with the reward of being given seed.

Ballplayers also associate a reward—successful performance—with prior behavior. If a player touches his crucifix and then gets a hit, he may decide the gesture was responsible for his good fortune and touch his crucifix the next time he comes to the plate. Unlike pigeons, however, most ballplayers are quicker to change their rituals once they no longer seem to work. Skinner found that once a pigeon associated one of its actions with the arrival of food or water, only sporadic rewards were necessary to keep the ritual going. One pigeon, believing that hopping from side to side brought pellets into its feeding cup, hopped ten thousand times without a pellet before finally giving up. But, then, didn't Wade Boggs eat chicken before every game, through slumps and good times, for seventeen years?

Obviously the rituals and superstitions of baseball do not make a pitch travel faster or a batted ball find the gaps between the fielders, nor do the Trobriand rituals calm the seas or bring fish. What both do, however, is give their practitioners a sense of control, and with that, added confidence. And we all

[2]Bronislaw Malinowski, *Magic, Science and Religion and Other Essays* (Glencoe, IL: Free Press, 1948).

[3]B. F. Skinner, *Behavior of Organisms: An Experimental Analysis* (New York: Appleton Century, 1938).

know how important that is. If you really believe eating chicken or hopping over the foul lines will make you a better hitter, it probably will.

Review Questions

1. According to Gmelch, what is magic, and why to people practice it?

2. What parts of baseball are most likely to lead to magical practice? Why?

3. What is meant by the terms *taboo* and *fetish?* Illustrate these concepts using examples from this article.

4. How are Malinowski's and Skinner's theories of magic alike and different? What is each designed to explain?

5. Can you think of other areas of U.S. life where magic is practiced? Do the same theories used in this article account for these examples, too?

Introduction and Review Questions reprinted from *Conformity and Conflict: Readings in Cultural Anthropology*, 12/e, Ed. James Spradley and David W. McCurdy, (2006), by permission of Allyn and Bacon.

6

The Genocidal State

Hutu Extremism and the Origins of the "Final Solution"
in Rwanda

Alex de Waal

Since taking his doctorate at Oxford, Alex de Waal has been involved with numerous NGOs (nongovernmental organizations) concerned with human rights, disaster relief, and development in Africa. He is the author of a definitive study on the Sudanese famine and co-director of the organization African Rights.

It is hard for simple reportage . . . to do justice to the bloodshed in Rwanda. What we need to do now—and what may, paradoxically, be easier—is to begin to explain it.

Elements of the story can be sought in desperate land pressure in Rwanda, in rural poverty intensified by the collapse of the international coffee price, and in the determination of a privileged coterie to retain their commanding positions in the Government and the army in the face of political and economic

Reprinted from the *London Times Literary Supplement*, July 1, 1994.

"readjustment" of the state. These have been fuel for the fire. But what ignited the genocide is an extremist racial ideology, an ideology that would be laughable were it not so demonically powerful.

Rwanda is more than another collapsing African state. The interim government of Rwanda is fighting for the right—as it sees it—to free itself from the moral claims of the rest of the world. This requires not just the eradication of the Tutsi minority but the annihilation of the human-rights and democracy movement in Rwanda, and all the values it stands for. In this furnace, extremist politicians are re-forging the identity of the Hutu people. It is frightening to watch.

To understand Hutu extremism one needs to delve into the origins of Hutu identity. Anthropologists and historians unite in deriding the description of Hutu and Tutsi as "tribes," and even as distinct "ethnic groups." The two speak the same language, share the same territory and traditional political institutions, and—despite caricatures to the contrary—it is often impossible to tell which group an individual belongs to on the basis of physical appearance. Rwanda is—or was—one of the true nations in Africa. A century ago, the colonists found a powerful and relatively centralized kingdom, consisting of three groups, determined largely by occupational status, and a large number of clans, determined by landholding. They were not even distinct "ethnic groups."

The European conquerors, first German and then Belgian, seized upon the occupational categorization, imbuing it with a hierarchical racial classification. The Tutsi minority were identified as a Hamitic aristocracy, who ruled a state of such sophistication that they could only have originated from a place, geographically, culturally and above all racially nearer Europe, that is, Ethiopia. Mgr Leon Classe, the first Roman Catholic Archbishop of Rwanda and the individual most responsible for shaping colonial policies there, considered the Tutsi to have an Aryan strain, while his acolytes claimed to have retrieved their origin as a lost tribe of Christendom. The "Hamitic hypothesis"—which holds that all pre-colonial civilization in Africa was brought by outsiders, specifically the Hamitic branch of the Caucasian race—is no longer academically respectable. But when the Tutsi courtiers converted to Roman Catholicism, abandoning the traditional sacral kingship that underpinned their authority, they seized upon it as legitimation for their continued rule.

Meanwhile, the Hutu majority were designated Bantu peasants, consigned to a life of toil and denied the possibility of education or a political role. This persisted until 1959, when, with independence approaching, the Belgians assisted in a "social revolution" that swept away the Tutsi monarchy and installed a Hutu republic. Both extremist politicians and many European missionaries still insist on talking of the "Huturace." Hutu politicians have turned the Hamitic hypothesis back in the face of their former masters: the Hutu now elevated to the original inhabitants, the Tutsi condemned as foreigners in their own country. (One reason why so many corpses have been washed into Lake Victoria is that a prominent ideologue, Dr Leon Mugesera, exhorted the population to return their erstwhile masters to Ethiopia, via the short cut of the Nyaborongo river.) The tiny group of Twa hunter-gatherers and potters were given the lowest status of all: aboriginal pygmies, a remnant of an earlier stage of human evolution. They remain one of the most despised and maltreated minorities in Africa.

It was common for European colonists to administer their territories through local intermediaries, creating or solidifying local oligarchies as they did so. Only in Rwanda and Burundi, however, was this overlaid with such an explicitly racial ideology. These two countries were also unusual in the extremes resorted to by the colonists. In the 1930s, the Belgians conducted a census and issued an identity card for each individual, which specified whether they were Tutsi, Hutu or Twa. Such was the slender basis for the racial typology that the census-takers were obliged to use ownership of cows as a criterion: those with ten or more were Tutsi, those with less were Hutu, in perpetuity. On the basis of a cow or two hinged the status of overlord or serf, and with it access to education and every other privilege bestowed by the administration. The cards still exist today—they are the means whereby the road-block militiamen know whom to kill and whom to spare.

As elsewhere in Africa, clan identity cuts across ethnicity. Each of Rwanda's fourteen major and numerous minor clans contains Tutsi, Hutu and Twa lineages. Before the late nineteenth century, social mobility across the categories was not uncommon. But Tutsi supremacy was cemented and extended, and "Tutsi" and "Hutu" became the most important political categories for Rwandese. This was most resented in north-west Rwanda, where the independent Hutu princedoms, known as Abahinza, were dismantled and Tutsi rulers imposed. Dr Ferdinand Nahimana, a leading Hutu extremist ideologue and Director of Radio-Télévision des Libres Mille Collines, whose radio broadcasts have been instrumental in inciting the killings, built his academic career at the National University of Rwanda on chronicling the Abahinza. His papers (for example, "Les Principautés Hutu du Rwanda Septentrional," in *La Civilization ancienne des peuples des Grands Lacs*, Paris 1979) appear in scholarly publications. President Juvenal Habyarimana, who died in the plane crash of April 6, and his lieutenants, who have since presided over the genocide, hail from this area and see themselves as the heirs of the Hutu princes.

Specialists on Rwanda protest in vain that Hutu and Tutsi are not separate ethnic groups. But sixty years of colonial and Tutsi rule, and thirty-five years of Hutu supremacy following the 1959 Revolution, which consigned half the Tutsi population to exile, have fundamentally changed the nature of the relationships between them. Political conflict, punctuated by intercommunal violence, has created distinct and mutually opposed Hutu and Tutsi identities, which, for all the hesitations of social scientists, are identifiably "ethnic."

Some insight into such processes of creating identity can be gleaned from the study of rather different, small-scale societies in south-west Ethiopia by David Turton, whose essay is the outstanding contribution to *Ethnicity and Conflict in the Horn of Africa*:

> If groups such as the Mursi are treated . . . as "given in nature," then the conflict which is seen to define their boundaries is also given in nature; it is simply the way

in which independent political groups must relate to each other in the absence of overarching political structure. But, if a network of relations based on clanship and other identities is treated as primary, conflict begins to look like the means whereby independent and mutually opposing political units are temporarily "carved out" from this "underlying" sociality in the first place.

This stands Hobbesian theory on its head; political organization, and ultimately states, are not what constrains the individual's propensity to violence, but what shapes it. Turton continues:

> I suggest that for the Mursi and their neighbours, warfare is not a means by which an already constituted political group seeks to defend or extend its territory, but a means by which the very idea of it as an independent political unit, free from the normative claims of outsiders, is created and kept alive.

In terms of human lives, this can be very costly. (Turton's analysis, developed over decades of familiarity with the Mursi, should be required reading for all who are involved in conflict resolution.)

Another paper in this collection, Tim Allen's account of the creation of ethnicity on the Sudan-Uganda border, charts a similar process whereby colonial administration, armed conflict and the popular currency of the notion of "tribe" have created the Acholi and Madi tribes, partly supplanting the more diffuse and complex relationships that existed beforehand. To argue that this tribes thus manufactured are artificial is to miss the point. As Allen points out, it is impossible to interpret recent events without recourse to tribal labels, and they are the labels used by the people themselves. Above all, people kill each other because of them.

Although derived from societies remote from centres of state power, the academic debate has insights for all concerned with the conundrum of the reinvigoration of nationalism and ethnic exclusivism. These are the currents tapped by politicians with a chauvinist agenda, and the resonances in Rwanda are compelling. On one side of the conflict are the leaders of the Tutsi-dominated Rwandese Patriotic Front (RPF). These are mostly children of refugees who fled to Uganda in 1959–63; their identities have been shaped by a generation of exile. Many fought as members of the Ugandan National Resistance Army (NRA) led by Yoweri Museveni, which captured Kampala and formed a government in 1986. Never fully accepted in Uganda, several thousand Rwandese members of the NRA deserted, formed the RPF, and invaded Rwanda on October 1, 1990.

Echoing their schooling at Makerere University, the RPF leaders complain that the ethnic labels Hutu and Tutsi are some sort of "mistake." They popularize this by harking back to the mythical origins of a unified Rwandese people unsullied by colonialism—conveniently skating over the Tutsi oppression of the Hutu in historical times. Their ideology has another intellectual lineage, traceable through the NRA to Frelimo in Mozambique, where Museveni first underwent training, and thence to Mao Tse-tung. Maoist theories of guerrilla war stress social transformation through participation in a liberation struggle, and focus on socio-economic tensions rather than ethnic solidarity. The RPF ideology is self-serving, designed for Western ears. Playing down ethnicity promotes the interests of a relatively wealthy and well-educated minority, and hides the enduring contempt many Tutsi commanders feel for the Hutu. Moreover, a display of military discipline strengthens the RPF's claim to dominate the future Rwandese army. But this politically cynical yet sociologically naive ideology has helped—so far—to prevent RPF soldiers wreaking a massive revenge on the Hutu populace.

On the other side, the Hutu racists regard the Hutu-Tutsi conflict as "given in nature," and repeatedly invoke the Hamitic-Bantu distinction. A Rwandan government pamphlet from 1990, entitled "The whole truth of the October 1990 war imposed upon Rwanda by the aggressors from Uganda armed forces," referring to President Museveni's origins in the "Hamitic" Hima people, enumerates "The true motives of the aggressors":

> [To] set up an extended Hima-Tutsi kingdom in the Bantu area of the Great-Lakes region. It should be recalled that in identification with the Aryan race, both ethnic groups consider themselves as being superior to other ethnic groups and use the swastika of Hitler as their symbol.

The last claim is wholly untrue, but this is mild in comparison with the propaganda put out in the Kinyarwanda language. Evidence that the extremists believed their own propaganda is contained in an internal Ministry of Defence memorandum from 1992, "Definition and identification of the enemy." Passing through "Tutsi refugees" and "Hutu who are hostile to the regime" the list concludes with "The Nilo-Hamitic people of the region." Ironically, this racial fantasy is underwritten by Tutsi supremacists in Burundi, the mirror-image neighbouring country where government and army remain dominated by the Tutsi minority. There, too, mutually antagonistic identities have been created and reinforced by colonial rule and politically instigated communal violence.

As well as a bid for power, the mass killing in Rwanda is a struggle to define the identity of the Rwandese Hutu. In *The Cohesion of Oppression*, Catherine Newbury argues that Hutu identity itself was a creation of the common experience of Rwandese peasants excluded from power and privilege during the colonial era. Before that, "hutu" merely referred to the status of vassal. Divided by clan, region and their relationship to the pre-colonial states and sub-states within Rwanda's colonial borders, Rwandese farmers became "Hutu" by default, as access to state power came to define the Tutsi.

Earlier scholars have charted the central role of the Christian missions in giving shape to this consciousness. Ian Linden's *Church and Revolution in Rwanda* (1977) is the classic of this literature. The Roman Catholic White Fathers, under Mgr Classe, formed a Tutsi state Church in the heyday of colonial rule. Later—partly because the Anglicans and Baptists began evangelizing the Hutu—the Catholic Church switched, in time to underwrite the creation of the Republic. The late Catholic Archbishop, Mgr Vincent Nsengiyumva, who was captured and killed by RPF forces last month, served on the Central Committee of Habyarimana's ruling party for fifteen years.

Newbury, deriving her account from a study of the south-west periphery of the kingdom, reveals how uneven the local experience of Tutsi rule was, challenging the previous orthodoxy that patron-client ties imbued the whole of Rwandese society. *The Cohesion of Oppression* is a valuable addition to the literature, running parallel to Linden's book in that its main aim is to explain the "social revolution" of 1959, a revolution that did indeed precisely reverse the political order.

Since then, Hutu politicians have ruled Rwanda. While still portraying the Hutu as downtrodden, they have used the same methods of ethnic discrimination to award the privileges of state power to themselves. A *coup* in 1973, announced by its leader, Major-General Habyarimana, as a "moral revolution," called a halt to anti-Tutsi pogroms and promised development without politics. But since 1990, with simultaneous economic crisis, populist mobilization for multi-party elections and the threat of the RPF, Hutu extremism has returned in a far more virulent form. The scholarly literature has yet to grapple with this.

Perhaps it is the very fact that Hutu ethnicity has such insubstantial foundations that compels the extremists to sharpen it, using methods that would be absurd were they not so inflammatory. The last few years have witnessed an outpouring of propaganda calling for no repetition of the "mistakes" of 1959, when the Tutsi were "allowed to escape" abroad. The message mixes traditional, religious and racial themes, often subverting them. For example, the third of the Hutu extremists' "Ten Commandments," published in 1990 in *Kangura*, a leading Rwandese newspaper, reads: "Are not [Hutu women] beautiful, good secretaries and more honest?" The sophisticated may laugh, but the list continues to number eight, "The Hutu should stop having mercy on the Tutsi" and number ten, "We shall consider a traitor any Hutu who will persecute his Hutu brother for having read, spread and taught this ideology."

The propagandists' principle of the bigger the lie, the greater the credulity, has been well observed. Peasants in areas overrun by the RPF are reportedly astonished that the Tutsi soldiers do not have horns, tails and eyes that glow in the dark—such is the content of the radio broadcasts they listen to. The terrorist principles perfected by Renamo are also in evidence: the symbolic inversion of moral values (churches and hospitals are favoured places for massacres) and forcing ordinary people to kill, so that they feel dehumanized and worthy only of the company of other killers.

The character of ethnicity in Rwanda presents the architect of genocide with another problem: how to distinguish his victims. It cannot be done by language or location, and—despite the best efforts of German and Belgian physical anthropologists—height and length of nose are uncertain guides. Checking identity cards is a time-consuming business, and the killers relied on speed for the success of their operation. The extremists solved this by mobilizing at least one militiaman from every ten households across the country, so that every Tutsi family could be pointed out by someone who knew them personally. Hence schoolchildren have been killed by their teachers, shopkeepers by their customers, neighbours by their neighbours.

Taking their name from the communal work groups that in the 1970s received the acclaim of aid agencies as the vanguard of equitable development, the militia are known as *interahamwe*, "those with a common goal." Mass murder masquerades as civic duty. Catechists wield machetes, and archbishops have defended the Government as "peace-loving." By these means, the interim government of Rwanda has succeeded in perfecting an intermediate technology of genocide. Using fragmentation grenades, machetes and big clubs with nails sticking out, they have matched the industrialized methods of extermination developed by the Nazis.

But the killing in Rwanda is more extreme still than genocide, and in this lies a second, complementary strand of an explanation. There is a third ideology at work in Rwanda—one that again has both local and international roots. This is "democratization" in its various forms: "conflict resolution," "human rights," "civil society" and "good governance."

In accordance with the extremists' tenth commandment, the first and most prominent victims of the killing were Hutu: opposition politicians, academics, journalists, human-rights activists, lawyers, priests, businessmen. The cream of the country's civil society was slaughtered in a few days by the Presidential Guard, who had earlier compiled their wanted lists. A curfew, imposed under the pretence that uncontrollable ethnic strife had broken out, enabled the soldiers to hunt down their victims in their homes. It was the ultimate *putsch:* physical liquidation of all advocates of democratization. Observers were confused because some of the victims were themselves members of the Government. Agatha Uwilingiyimana, killed on the first day along with ten Belgian soldiers from the United Nations who were her guards, was both Prime Minister and an opposition politician. Her position reflects a deep irony, for, until April 6, Rwanda was a model for a transition to democracy and the peaceful resolution of armed conflict.

In 1990, President Habyarimana bowed to the "democracy wave" sweeping Africa and agreed to move from a single-party to a multi-party system. In the same year he also faced the RPF invasion. International pressure brought both sides to the negotiating table, and a series of accords were hammered out. Under close monitoring by the United Nations, cabinet posts were to be shared with the opposition, the police retrained, the national army and the rebel front merged and scaled down, and free elections held. Regional powers such as Tanzania and Zaire played a role, the Belgians backed the agreements, and a United Nations force was dispatched to demonstrate the commitment of the world.

Whenever Habyarimana prevaricated or stalled on the timetable to democracy, the international peace-brokers stepped in and forced him to keep his word. A desperate attempt by Hutu extremists to derail the process by assassinating a leading opposition politician on February 21 unleashed several days of violence by the *interahamwe* militia. But the UN, the Organization of African Unity and Rwanda's main Western donors did not flinch: Habyarimana was dragged back to the negotiating table, and forced to agree. Under countervailing pressure from his hardline coterie, he tried to wriggle again; the regional leaders called him for a conference in Dar es Salaam. The President was forced to agree once more: the transitional institutions would be set up. He left for home in his personal plane, but word of his latest capitulation had reached the Presidential Guard stationed near Kigali airport, and they shot him down.

Habyarimana was a victim of the international peace industry as well as of the hardliners he had hand-picked for the Presidential Guard. The peace process had failed to bring an important (albeit nasty) section of Rwandese society along with it. At times, those guiding the international diplomacy seemed to be closing their eyes and wishing the extremists away.

Before April 6, Rwanda had one of the most vigorous human-rights movements in Africa. Six independent human-rights organizations cooperated in exposing abuses by government and rebel forces. They also invited an International Commission of Inquiry, consisting of ten human-rights experts from around the world. The Commission visited Rwanda in 1993 and compiled a comprehensive and courageous report, documenting violations and naming those responsible—including senior members of the Government and army and extremist ideologues. Habyarimana was reported to have personally acquiesced to a massacre, with a nod of his head, in 1992.

Democracy implied justice. The individuals named were promised an amnesty, but knew that their actions were under scrutiny. Their strategy to escape justice was to kill all those who had collaborated in human-rights investigations. They killed most of them. It is a shocking reminder of just how high the stakes are in the human-rights business. There was plentiful evidence for preparations for mass killing. The UN Special Envoy publicly objected to the arming of militias on several occasions, and the names of the leaders of the "Zero Network" death squads were circulated by the civil opposition. But no contingency plans were made. This was particularly shortsighted because of the example of Burundi the previous year.

The democratization process in Burundi reached fruition in June 1993, with the election of Melchior Ndadaye as the first Hutu President. Entirely carried through by Burundis themselves, it was a shining example of peaceful transition—as one observer put it, "too good to be true." But, with their position under threat, on October 21 the Tutsi-controlled army mounted a *coup d'état,* assassinated Ndadaye, and unleashed communal violence that killed up to 50,000 people. The international community reacted immediately to condemn the *putsch:* there was to be no foreign aid or diplomatic recognition unless the extremists backed down. The extremists duly returned to barracks (where they have been left undisturbed); and since then Burundi has been in a fragile state of power-sharing interrupted by sporadic assassinations.

When the storm erupted in Rwanda, the reaction of the Western world was merely to decry the anarchic savagery, evacuate its citizens, and pull out all but a handful of UN troops. Under this smokescreen the killers proceeded undisturbed; and the local human-rights activists were left to their fate. Since then, the pace of the diplomatic ball-game has been much slower than the momentum of the genocide. The UN Commission for Human Rights has met in extraordinary session and appointed a Special Rapporteur, but criminal indictments for genocide are still in the distant future. The foreign minister of the interim government was allowed to deliver a racist diatribe to the UN Security Council—no one even considered changing the diplomatic rules to prevent the advocacy of genocide at the UN's inner sanctum. In Kigali, the UN Special Envoy is still grasping at the standard formulas: ceasefire and political settlement. Maintaining "neutrality" by blaming both sides equally, he is apparently oblivious to the impossibility of an agreement between a government whose *raison d'être* is genocide, and a rebel force that will not stop its advance until it has saved every remaining Tutsi from the threat of the militias. It seems probable that the genocide will be resolved in time-honoured fashion—either the killers will run out of victims, or the rebel army will win the war. International troops sent with the wrong mandate—for example, to impose a ceasefire—will be a practical and moral irrelevance.

This should be giving sleepless nights to the advocates of peace and democracy in the United Nations, Western embassies and humanitarian foundations. Their own ideologues are spectacularly unable to deal with political philosophies such as Hutu extremism. For example, Ronald Cohen's keynote chapter in *Human Rights and Governance in Africa* persists in seeing the weakness of the state as the reason for ethnic conflict, even citing earlier rounds of killings in Rwanda and Burundi as an example of this. This is unreconstructed Hobbes: the "great beast" of popular violence must be constrained by a contract between the individual and the state.

Articulating an evolutionary view with similar credentials to the Hamitic hypothesis, Cohen argues in passing that ascribed rights based on race or ethnicity "can be predicted to atrophy over time." It is perhaps unfair to characterize the whole of a solid collection on the basis of a few remarks in one paper, but the student who reads the publisher's claims for "timeliness" and "originality" will be disappointed. Though the publication date is 1993, the papers for this volume were written in 1988. The Rwandese method of genocide was perfected in less time than it took for the proceedings of an academic conference on human rights to reach the publisher's catalogue.

Generals and genocidal ideologues continue to sharpen their tools faster than the proponents of peace and democracy. While human-rights advocates and relief agencies still shudder in shock from Rwanda, dictators are observing closely how the crime unfolds. Some, no doubt, have more than a little admiration for the sheer audacity of the Hutu extremists' attempted "final solution" to the threat of political opposition. If interim President Theodor Sindikubabwo, Major-General Augustine Bizimana, Dr Casimir Bizimungu and their coterie succeed—if they retain a stake in power, and remain legitimate interlocutors in the eyes of the international diplomatic corps—that will be an advertisement for mass political killing, and an open invitation for others to replicate it.

More is at stake in Rwanda even than the survival of the Tutsi people. The killers' aim is a "final solution" to the threat to their power and beliefs posed by human rights and democracy itself. Should they succeed, the armoury of political extremism worldwide will be enriched with a host of new techniques for propagandizing and swiftly executing mass murder, as well as methods of confusing, neutralizing and even co-opting the international peace industry. Should the killers fail, it will almost certainly be due to the few thousand guerrillas of the RPF, not to the troops of the UN or any other international pressure: an accidental defeat for genocide, not a victory for human rights.

Scholars, lawyers and diplomats expend huge energies refining the instruments and expanding the institutions of international human rights. But this community, too, is ultimately defined by the battles it fights. Should it refuse to enter the fray in Rwanda, it will be diminished. For a movement that ultimately depends on collective moral authority, this would be profoundly discouraging.

7

Nomads on Notice

Daniel Stiles

Daniel Stiles received a Ph.D. from the University of California at Berkeley for work on prehistoric cultures of eastern and southern Africa and is now a consultant to the United Nations Environmental Programme. He is also a research associate at the British Institute in East Africa. He first met the Gabbra in 1971 when working as a student archaeological assistant at Richard Leakey's research site on Lake Turkana. His current interest is in food foragers of Kenya, Madagascar, and India who are suppliers of forest products; his hope is to use this economic importance as a means for saving biological and cultural diversity.

Northern Kenya is a land of extremes, with wind-blasted volcanic wastes in the lowlands and lush tropical forests on isolated mountains. The territory is divided among several tribes that vigilantly defend their domains. The Gabbra pastoralists, who number about 35,000, cluster around the cracked, salt-encrusted mud flats of the Chalbi Desert and along the eastern shore of Lake Turkana. Because rainfall is sporadic and localized, water sources and vegetation

Reprinted from *Natural History* 9 (1993). Copyright © 1993 by the American Museum of Natural History.

are scattered and unpredictable. (Oases near the lake often provide fresh water, but the jade-colored lake itself is bitter with accumulated salts.) The Gabbra must move periodically, often splitting up their camps to take advantage of nature's meager offerings.

The keys to the Gabbra's survival are mobility, hard work, and cooperation. During their lives, married men go through various life stages, becoming at different times "political elders" and then "ritual elders." Along with those chosen for specific leadership roles, these elders control Gabbra life and also provide moral guidance.

The Gabbra separate their herds of camels, cattle, sheep, and goats by species, age, and whether or not they are giving milk. Milk is the traditional staple, followed by meat and then blood, but the Gabbra now commonly buy cornmeal through the sale of small livestock. They keep milk-giving animals at the main settlements (*ola*) and, to avoid overgrazing, send the dry ones and most males off to distant locations. Because of the danger of raiding by other tribes, young warriors usually run the satellite camps, called *fora*. The zones separating enemy tribes are sparsely inhabited.

One of the insecure zones is around Koobi Fora, paleontologist Richard Leakey's research site. In 1971, while I was there on my first trip to northern Kenya, a raiding party of a neighboring nomadic group, the Dassenech, came across the border from Ethiopia, sending the Gabbra running and scaring the wits out of the researchers and camp crew. The Dassenech had guns; the Gabbra didn't.

In a few hours, the Gabbra can pack a settlement, tents and all, on the backs of their camels and be on their way to an area where rain has fallen. The household effects are simple: aluminum cooking pots; wooden and woven fiber containers for storing milk, meat, and fat; bed poles and sleeping skins; and various ritual sticks that symbolize status (for a young man, a married man, a father, a married woman, an elder, and so on). Between 6:30 and 11:30 one morning, I observed four women in an area called Bubissa pack up their four families' skin tents, along with their pole frameworks and assorted contents, and load them onto the backs of groaning camels. The four households then set off on camels across the stony plains to go to Maikona, a two-day walk. A settlement may move up to ten times a year, depending on grazing conditions and security.

The Gabbra define four seasons, according to temperature and rainfall. Although conditions vary from year to year, generally the long, heavy rains come between late March and early June, followed by the cool dry season from June to September. Short rains arrive in October and last until early December, when the hot dry season sets in. During the dry periods, the Gabbra tend to live in small settlements grouped around permanent water sources, while in wetter times they occupy larger, more widely scattered settlements. When water becomes available in rain pools, for example, the otherwise dry Huri Hills become a favored pasture area. Three times a year, as many family members as possible, together with their livestock, gather at the *ola* for a *sorio*, a ceremony to bless the community and the livestock and to pray for rain and fertility.

Camels make up the bulk of the tribe's holdings, and without them the Gabbra could not live where they do. As beasts of burden, camels enable the Gabbra to move the *ola* rapidly to find fresh pasture after a cloudburst. Camels also transport water to the settlement, permitting an *ola* to be situated in good pasture as much as thirty miles from water. The Gabbra prefer to have female camels, with as many lactating ones as possible. In dry lands, camels provide much more milk than cattle do, lactating on average for at least a year after bearing a calf. A good camel can give more than two and a half gallons of milk a day during the rainy season and two to five quarts during the dry season. In contrast, a typical cow lactates only seven to nine months, giving two quarts of milk a day when pasture is lush and just a pint a day—and eventually none at all—during the dry times.

Camels also do less damage to the environment than other livestock. Their soft feet do not scuff up top-soil, causing it to blow or wash away, as hoofs do; and they feed on various types of vegetation, particularly leaves, so that the land does not lose the soil-conserving grass. Owing to the camel's relatively varied diet, its milk is higher in vitamin C and certain other nutrients than cattle milk.

Despite their sense of separate identity, the Gabbra are of mixed origins, in part derived from neighboring peoples. Arriving in the region in the late nineteenth century, mainly from Ethiopia and from farther east in Kenya, they took the land they now occupy from the Rendille and Samburu, who were squeezed to the south. They have since defended their territory successfully against invasions by the Turkana, who live west of Lake Turkana, and the Masai, who once occupied much of central and southern Kenya.

The Gabbra retain a reputation as fierce warriors. In greeting and prayer, however, they often use the word *nagaya*—"peace"—a cultural trait they share with Semitic peoples of western Asia, who are members of the same Afro-Asiatic language family. They particularly abhor strife within the tribe. I once witnessed two children, a boy and a girl, get into a fight. The boy hit the girl on the head with a rock and knocked her down. While I was treating her wound with antiseptic, several adults ran around seemingly in a panic. By the time I had finished and calmed the girl down, the parents had organized an expiation ceremony on the spot. They recited prayers and sacrificed a sheep offered by the boy's parents. I received a goatskin bracelet made from the sacrificed animal, signifying welcome and peace.

Water is critical for survival in the desert, but the Gabbra carefully avoid fighting among themselves over access to the few wells and water holes. At the height of the dry season, hundreds of thirsty camels, cattle, sheep, and goats may bellow for water and kick up clouds of dust around a well as their herders struggle to keep them at bay and await their allotted turn. The "father of dividing," selected by the political elders (and almost always one himself), schedules each herd by species and ownership. He must be a man of fairness and iron will.

A chain of six or eight men position themselves in the well on dug-out ledges, projecting rocks in the wall, or scaffolding and pass the traditional giraffeskin containers up and down. The wells are often called "singing wells" because the men keep up a rhythmic chant as they draw the water up by hand from a depth of as much as fifty feet. The animals drink from a trough of molded mud, which needs constant repair from the damage caused by their jostling.

One of the biggest problems the Gabbra face is fulfilling labor needs. Averaging the wet- and dry-season regimes, researchers have calculated that nine people must work nine hours a day, every day, to mind one family herd and take care of the various household chores. To find the necessary labor, the Gabbra draw on a network of kinship and other social ties to look after the subdivided herds at the *ola* and the outlying camel, cattle, and small livestock camps.

In doing censuses, I learned that many more people are attached to a household than mom, dad, and the kids. For example, Wario Guyo, his wife, Shanu, and their young daughter slept in their house, while Wario's two nephews and an unmarried brother-in-law slept behind a thorn-branch windbreak out by the camel corral. A man belonging to a lower-status subgroup, the Wata, not allowed by tradition to sleep in the *ola,* lived to the west in the shade of an acacia tree. These additional household members each had a different herd of Wario's to care for and were paid in kind by food and stock offspring. Away from the *ola,* which was located on the eastern margin of the Chalbi Desert, two of Wario's sons looked after a *fora* near Lake Turkana, and the third was in school at Mount Marsabit, about sixty miles away.

To discover how many animals people owned, I had to unravel various types of loans and ownership arrangements. One young married man, Dub Boru, explained that most of his animals still belonged to his father, and that he had received them as an advance on his inheritance. He also had three camels and several sheep and goats that his *abuya,* a special uncle, had given him on important occasions, such as his circumcision. Dub also managed several milk camels obtained on loan. In exchange for taking care of the animals, he was entitled to their milk and their offspring, but had to give all subsequent generations of animals to the owner. Counting all the animals at Dub's *ola* and out at the *fora,* I estimated that he controlled at least eight lactating camels, two lactating cows, ten other adult camels, seven camel calves, four other cattle, and about sixty sheep and goats (small livestock reproduce quickly and are often sold or slaughtered, so exact figures are hard to come by). These animals provided food for six adults and adolescents and eight children.

Dub also exchanged animals. When his second child was born, for example, he traded one of his transport camels for a lactating cow; and when he needed money for cloth for his wife and school fees for a sister's son, he traded a heifer camel for ten goats, which he then sold. (Gabbra do not sell camels directly for money, for they fear this would bring misfortune.) Even with these maneuverings, Dub's animals weren't always sufficient to feed his family, owing to fluctuations in milk supply. So he pooled his herd with that of his brother-in-law, who was in a similar situation. The combined herds provided a more reliable source of milk.

The right of personal ownership does not, in the Gabbra's view, permit a man to monopolize more animals than he and his dependents need for survival. Through loans and gifts, excess animals are redistributed to the needy, allowing the whole community to survive. The secular authority of political elders and the moral authority of ritual elders ensure that these mechanisms of social cooperation are respected. One old man, Guracha Galgallo, is famous for owning about one thousand camels and many cattle and small livestock. Yet he dresses as all other Gabbra do, lives in the same style house, and eats the same food as the poorest Gabbra (although probably more regularly). Most of his animals are out on loan to those who have need of milk or transport or a bull for mating. His reward is respect.

The redistribution of livestock maximizes their use for food, transport, and cash. When there is a real surplus of animals, more than needed to meet the food requirements for the community as a whole (a rare occurrence), they are sacrificed and consumed at special ceremonial occasions to thank Waqa, the supreme being. As a result, the burden placed on the fragile environment is kept to a minimum. In contrast, many cattle pastoralists with more restricted systems of redistribution accumulate great numbers of animals. While their herds serve as insurance against drought and other calamities, they can cause serious land degradation.

Because food is usually in short supply, the Gabbra store little, although they have the technology to do so. For example, milk is soured and made into a kind of yogurt that lasts for weeks. And pieces of meat, stored with fat in small woven or wooden containers, can keep for more than a year. With food resources fluctuating from season to season and year to year, a group must manage enough animals to survive the worst conditions. To get by, an average family of six needs about twenty-eight camels, including six to eight that are lactating, or the equivalent in other cattle. Unfortunately, in 1991 drought and an undiagnosed camel disease reduced the herds below this level.

When the Gabbra and other northern Kenya pastoralists experienced hard times in the past, they always managed to endure. But now they are receiving food relief, and foreign relief agencies and other Westerners are exerting great influence on them. Because of the scarcity of livestock—and deteriorating security due to the troubles in Somalia and Ethiopia—raiding has also become much more frequent. Some Gabbra have moved to refugee camps to escape armed bandits.

If the neighboring countries regain political stability, and if the rains return, the Gabbra's traditional life should improve. But the last time I visited Gabbra country, I was not encouraged. Outsiders—famine relief workers, development-aid workers, missionaries, teachers, and government officers—are telling the Gabbra that they are backward and primitive. They are urging some to move to settlements on nearby Mount Marsabit and learn how to grow crops. There they would join Ethiopian immigrants, mission-settled refugees, southern Kenyan traders and administrators, and others who are encroaching on a "protected" national park forest.

Most Gabbra I know are horrified at the thought of taking up cultivation. One man, a ritual elder named Elema Arbu, told me that becoming a farmer was equivalent to becoming an outcast. "Without livestock, how can I provide bride price for my sons? How can I pay my stock debts? How can I make *sorio* and other sacrifices? How can I give the stock gifts at my nephews' circumcisions? Without herds, how can I hold my head up?"

8

Witchcraft in Anthropological Perspective

Isak Niehaus

Isak Niehaus received his Ph.D. from the University of Witwatersrand and is a senior lecturer in the department of anthropology at the University of Pretoria in South Africa. He is the author of Witchcraft, Power and Politics: Exploring the Occult in the South African Lowveld.

Europeans and North Americans often regard the belief in witchcraft as unique to the witch persecutions of the Inquisition and Reformation. Whereas there was profound skepticism about witchcraft in early medieval Europe, this entire religious milieu changed with the Crusades and the Reformation. Witchcraft beliefs became enshrined in the theology of the church, and clergy assigned the

Reprinted from *Talking About People: Readings in Cultural Anthropology,* Third Edition, edited by William A. Haviland and Luis Vivanco (2002), The McGraw-Hill Companies.

administration of evil to Satan and witches. Since Satan was believed to be spiritual, he could only acquire physical bodies in which to do his work by entering people through possession. Otherwise Satan signed pacts with them to do as they were bid in return for mundane considerations (Parrinder 1963; Thomas 1971).

These changes precipitated the Inquisition, during which thousands of suspects were tried on charges of witchcraft, heresy, and devil worship by secular and ecclesiastical courts. As confessions were obtained voluntarily or wrung from the accused by torture, the belief in witchcraft attained greater credibility. A papal bull issued in 1484 by Pope Innocent VII identified witches as the prime enemy of the church. Three years later the book *Malleus Maleficarum* ("hammer of the witches") was published as a sort of handbook on the discovery, trail, torture, and execution of witches; it came to be used by Catholic and Protestant clergy throughout Europe. Passages were cited from the Scriptures—for example, "Thou shalt not suffer a witch to live," which is from Exodus. At least 300,000 witches were publicly executed at the stake.

Although the Reformation was partly a reaction against the Inquisition, Protestants did not halt witch persecutions. In fact, Geneva, Calvin's native city, became a center for witch-hunting. Clergy blamed Geneva's many disease epidemics on witches whom Satan allegedly incited to spread the plague. Large numbers of men and women were apprehended for making pacts with Satan and were accordingly tortured and burnt. These beliefs were also prevalent among Calvinists in Scotland and in New England; in 1692, two hundred suspected witches were arrested in Salem, Massachusetts. Of these, nineteen were hanged and one other was hounded to death (Boyer and Nissenbaum 1974). The reasons behind Calvinism's fear of witchcraft include the propagation of a dualistic worldview, a belief in the inevitability of sin, and the literal interpretation of biblical texts.

Actually, witchcraft beliefs are much more widely distributed in time and place. They are encountered throughout history on virtually all continents—in native North America, South America, Africa, Asia, and in the Pacific—and continue to be an important feature of contemporary times. Hunter-gatherers such as the Bushmen and Australian aboriginals are exceptional in that they do not believe in witchcraft. Due to its widespread distribution, witchcraft has become a staple topic of anthropological research.

Defining Witchcraft

In his famous study of the Azande of Anglo-Egyptian Sudan, Evans-Pritchard (1937) distinguished between "witchcraft" and "sorcery" by their technique. He defined the former as an innate, inherited ability to cause people misfortune or to kill them. For Azande, witchcraft involves unconscious psychic powers, and it emanates from an oval black swelling, located near the liver. By contrast, Azande referred to sorcery as the performance of rituals, the uttering of spells, and the manipulation of organic substances such as herbs, with the conscious intent of causing harm.

Middleton and Winter (1963) find Evans-Pritchard's distinction appropriate for east Africa, and Stephen (1986) insists that it illuminates the situation in many Melanesian societies. However, Turner (1964) shows that the distinction between "witchcraft" and "sorcery" is not made in the largest part of Africa, nor in many other parts of the world. Following Turner and many contemporary authors, I use the terms *witch* and *witchcraft* more broadly to denote both types of persons and modes of action. (In this review I retain the word *sorcery* only where it is used by the authors in the original texts.)

In an overview of several ethnographic studies, Mayer points to the recurrence of identical details, common to witchcraft beliefs nearly everywhere.

1. Though human, witches incorporate nonhuman power. Witches are possessed by Satan, have pythons in their bellies, work with animals such as snakes, cats, baboons, and owls, which they own as familiars, or themselves change into the shape of animals.
2. Witches are nearly always adults, who are said to inherit their destructive power. They may bear physical stigmata like a red eye, a devil's mark, or a special witchcraft substance.
3. Witches tend to become socially important in times of crisis, when all sorts of misfortune—sickness, death, drought, or plague—are ascribed to them.
4. Witches harm their own kin and neighbors rather than strangers. For example, residents of the South African lowveld believe that no witch can cross a river.
5. Witchcraft is motivated by envy and malice, rather than by the pursuit of material gain.
6. Witches reverse usual expectations of behavior. For example, they may stand backward when they knock on doors, ride baboons facing the tail, and negate all Christian values during the witches' Sabbath. Witches work at night, commit incest, practice cannibalism, and go naked instead of clothed.
7. Witchcraft is nearly always immoral.

Classical Anthropological Theories of Witchcraft

Anthropologists have generally left open questions about the actual performance of witchcraft. While some people may perform (or at least attempt to perform) witchcraft, even the most optimistic fieldworker does not expect to see people flying around on brooms. Rather, the classical anthropological theories of witchcraft by Fortune, Kluckhohn, Evans-Pritchard, and Marwick seek to unearth the social and psychological realities underlying witchcraft beliefs and the cultural meanings they encode.

Fortune (1932) analyzed "sorcery" on the island of Dobu, Melanesia, as a conception of mystical power. Here small exogamous villages were the basic political and territorial units, and clusters of equal villages formed endogamous localities that united for purposes of warfare. Dobuans made allegations of sorcery against their allies in war, whom they married, rather than against outsiders with whom they waged war (p. 35). Fortune argues that these allegations expressed tensions, resulting from conflicting solidarities between the *susu* (a matrilineal group of brothers, sisters, and sisters' children) and the marital group (comprising the husband, wife, and children). Moreover, because of rules of alternate residence, each Dobuan village sheltered a heterogeneous collection of "men of different village alliances who distrust each other thoroughly" (p. 9). He suggests that in such a political system—with no rank or titular authority—Dobuans perceived prowess in sorcery as a component of leadership and power. They conducted life as a covert series of night battles in which individuals used sorcery to assert themselves at the expense of others. According to Fortune, Dobuans used sorcery "for collecting bad debts and enforcing economic obligation, in vendetta to avenge one's own sickness or one's kinsmen's death, to wipe out any serious insult" (p. 175).

Evans-Pritchard (1937) demonstrated how witchcraft formed an "ideational system" among the Azande of Anglo-Egyptian Sudan. From the point of view of the individual, in particular situations, he argued, the beliefs presented a logical explanation of unfortunate events. Evans-Pritchard insisted that witchcraft beliefs supplemented theories of natural causation. They did not exclude empirical knowledge of cause and effect but provided answers to the particularity of misfortunes. He cites the famous example of a granary that collapses, injuring those sitting beneath it. The Azande could explain this event in empirical terms: termites had eaten the supports. According to this explanation, the fact that people sat beneath the granary when it collapsed was purely coincidental. However, the theory of witchcraft links these events. It explains why these particular people sat under the particular granary at the particular moment that it collapsed.

Kluckhohn (1944) elaborated a psychological theory of witchcraft. He insists that among the Navaho, witchcraft served as a channel for projecting emotions of guilt, desire, and aggression. By investing the witch with responsibility for misfortune, Navaho absolved themselves of blame. Their forbidden desires, such as incest, also found an outlet in fantasies of witchcraft. Moreover, under stressful conditions, witches were scapegoats for hostile impulses. The rigid rules of decorum among the Navaho allow little means for expression of hostility, except through accusations of witchcraft. Such accusations funnel pent-up negative emotions against individuals, without upsetting the wider society. Accusations of witchcraft also permit the direct expression of hostile feelings against people to whom one would otherwise be unable to express anger or enmity.

In his influential analysis of witchcraft beliefs and accusations among the Chewa of Northern Rhodesia (now Zambia), Marwick (1965) draws on sociological theories of conflict. He contends that witchcraft accusations reformulated problematic social relations that were not susceptible to judicial processes. Marwick found that 60 percent of sorcery accusations occurred within the matrilineage. As the matrilineage grew beyond the size that its resources could sustain, tensions over inheritance and succession became apparent. The leaders of different matrilineal segments then jockeyed for position and often attempted to discredit their rivals by accusing them of sorcery. In retrospective accounts, sorcery justified segmentation. It served as an idiom for initiating processes of fission and enabled the accusers to break off redundant relations and to discard unwanted obligations. Marwick (1965) notes that sorcery accusations were absent in the case of conjugal relations, because hostilities between spouses could easily be expressed and redressed by alternative means. The Chewa could attribute misfortune at home to the transgression of taboos, and the courts could easily dismantle conjugal relations by granting divorce.

Since the 1970s two different approaches have predominated in the study of witchcraft. On the one hand neo-Marxists demonstrated the instrumentality of witchcraft in political economic struggles. For example, Steadman sees the killing of witches by the Hewa of Papua New Guinea as an outcome of competition for resources between different roofing and flooring parties. By executing the members of other parties who threatened their interests, the witch killers generated fear and communicated their capacity to use violence to protect their interests. On the other hand, interpretive studies delineated the meanings of witchcraft beliefs within wider conceptual terms. In this tradition, Kelly (1976) shows that there is an analogical relation between witchcraft and sexual intercourse among the Etoro of New Guinea. He contends that the Etoro perceived both acts as transmitting life forces from one person to another. In witchcraft, the witch appropriates the victim's life forces to acquire added strength and vigor. Likewise, men suffer weakness and eventually death through the depletion of their semen, in which their life forces are concentrated. Women are the agents of this depletion and men the beneficiaries.

The Modernity of Witchcraft

Witchcraft beliefs and accusations are far from an archaic tradition that has disappeared with the growth of knowledge, modernization, and development. Recent studies show that modernization itself spawns new forms of witchcraft and that the occult has flourished precisely in the most modern sectors of society—such as sports, institutions of formal learning, politics, and new forms of entrepreneurship. There are deep anxieties throughout Africa and Melanesia about new forms of witchcraft that are reproducing on an increased scale. Indeed, the "modernity" of witchcraft has become a decidedly popular theme in anthropological studies since the 1990s (Comaroff and Comaroff 1993; Lattas 1993; Ciekawy and Geschiere 1998; Geschiere 1997). These studies subvert the certainties of the unilineal modernist scheme and highlight the inconsistencies and ambiguities of the modern.

Ciekawy and Geschiere contend that because witchcraft is so open-ended it becomes an obvious discourse for interpreting modern changes to linking local realities directly with global changes. "Witchcraft discourse forces an opening in the village and the closed family network: after all, it is the basic interests of the witch to betray his or her victims to outsiders" (Ciekawy and Geschiere 1998:5). They argue that it is through the opening of witchcraft that people or resources are withdrawn from the local community and disappear into the outer world. Hence, witchcraft is about "transgression and constantly redefining boundaries" (Ciekawy and Geschiere 1998:5). Not only do witchcraft discourses enable people to conceptualize the way in which the opening up of local communities has been accelerated by new technologies of transport and communication, but they also express people's concern about the selectivity of the opportunities and benefits that these processes provide.

Lattas (1993) shows how these processes are apparent in Papua New Guinea. He suggests that among the Kaliai of New Britain sorcery constitutes a kind of political language, containing a cultural critique of colonialism. He shows how powerful institutions such as the state and church are conceived of as fusing with the powers of indigenous sorcerers. Because the colonial state prevented reprisals against sorcerers the Kaliai perceived whites as somehow complicit in sorcery and as providing Melanesian sorcerers with a license to kill (p. 56). They argued that sorcerers supervised government cash crop projects, magistrates used the powers of sorcery to travel to different villages and to extract fines, and the Catholic Church destroyed its opponents by magic. Moreover, the Kaliai believed that sorcerers incorporate European symbols, offices, and commodities. People were said to learn and swap sorcery skills on the plantations and to purchase sorcery substances such as a very powerful herbicide on the marketplace. In this way "a violent space of death" "grows alongside, and is coextensive with commodity production" (p. 59). Moreover, dreams reveal Europeans as inhabiting Melanesian sorcery shrines.

Focusing on the Cameroon, Geschiere (1997) contends that witchcraft plays a vital role in modern politics and that rumors of witchcraft have overrun all political spaces, from village communities to the highest affairs of the nation-state. Colonial chiefs, educated elites, and modern politicians alike are purported to command occult forces called *djambe*. These forces even explain the superior rhetorical prowess of notables in the chiefly councils. *Djambe*—a small being that lives in a person's belly—transcends the opposition between good and evil. It is possessed by all and is the principle behind all success. *Djambe* can be used both constructively and destructively. At night a witch's *djambe* flies out to attack its victims. There were definite parallels between the lack of transparency and capriciousness of President Ahidjo's autocratic one-party system and the occult world of witchcraft, where actors and their acts are hidden from view. President Biya's multiparty democracy brought about political debate in all villages, but also greater insecurity, which made villagers resort to supernatural protection. Like conspiracy theories, witchcraft renders political processes and events comprehensible.

New forms of wealth, too, have found expression in witchcraft discourses. Sons of the villagers, who occupy important positions in the bureaucracy, act as brokers between clients in their home villages and the repressive state. In this context witchcraft constitutes a "popular mode of political action" against reticent urbanites who fail to further the interests of villagers. Rumors in Cameroon also denounce the nouveaux riches as a new brand of witches who transform their victims into zombies in order to get rich through exploiting their labor. Local witches are now supposed to work together with the mafia, organizing a worldwide zombie traffic in which Mt. Kupe—of old the place where zombies were taken—has become no more than a "relay station."

Geschiere (1997) shows that the state is experimenting with new ways of containing witchcraft. Since the 1970s regional courts in Cameroon's East Province have sentenced witches to terms of imprisonment for up to ten years, purely on the basis of testimony provided by certified *nkong* (diviners). Those convicted are poorer persons, deemed to present an anti-modern threat to progress. He sees this initiative as a logical outcome of the state's "hegemonic project," which aims to secure dominance over all domains of society, including the occult. (Also see Fisiy 1998.)

Witchcraft in the West

Witchcraft does not belong merely to former Third World countries and to the early beginnings of the modern European and North American world. As Cardozo (1972) and Steadman (1985) point out, the parallels between witchcraft and U.S. senator Joseph McCarthy's dreams about Red agents is indeed a close one. Moreover, Jean and John Comaroff point to a cluster of images in the popular culture of North America that address the contradictions of advanced capitalist societies: the "Fatal Attraction" of the corporate harridan who would destroy the home, husband, and family—and will not die; the dangerous market woman of Wall Street who will consume all before her, including the honest "Working Girl"; and the callous babyminder whose "Hand . . . Rocks the Cradle" and aborts social reproduction (Comaroff and Comaroff 1993:xxviii).

Witchcraft beliefs assume an even more concrete form in many Mediterranean societies, where it is believed that the envy of certain persons can bring harm to their objects through envy and an "evil eye." Envy and the evil eye are invoked to explain recurrent, persistent, and vague illnesses that doctors cannot cure, rather than obvious physical injuries or illness (Delamont 1995). The aggressors either caste the evil eye deliberately or do so unintentionally. Stewart (1991) reports that shepherds in Naxos, Greece, saw the evil eye as a "projectile of envy" that can strike a person, animal, or even valuable possessions such as television sets or motor bikes (p. 232). Victims were diagnosed by dropping oil into water—if it congulated, an evil eye had been at work. Once a diagnosis had been made, Naxiotes removed the evil eye by saying a prayer invoking the Trinity and by dropping a cross into a glass of water and then sprinkling the bubbles of water from the cross onto themselves. In the Portuguese town of Vila Branca, amulets were fixed around the garments of babies, the sign of the cross was painted onto the houses of both the bride and groom before a wedding, and curers could lift the evil eye from its victims (Lawrence 1982).

When Favret-Saada did fieldwork in Brocage, an area in the northwest of France, between 1968 and 1971, she found that peasants did not want to discuss witchcraft with her. To talk about witchcraft with intellectuals from Paris would label them as backward and could endanger them because witches do not like their victims talking about witchcraft. To do so would render them liable to insanity. Jean Barbin—an impotent alcoholic whose cows had brucellosis—was convinced that a malevolent neighbor had bewitched him. Barbin fixed on Favret-Saada as an unwitcher, whose task it was to take the witchcraft and send it back onto the witch. If that works, only the witch suffers. But if the unwitcher is not strong enough, the witchcraft can leave the original victim and attack him or her instead. As long as Favret-Saada did not believe in the existence of witchcraft, she could act (or pretend to act) as an unwitcher. However, she eventually began to believe that witchcraft was a better explanation of Barbin's impotence than anything orthodox psychiatry could offer and found herself believing that the witchcraft had indeed been diverted from Jean Barbin to her. She began to experience a series of inexplicable accidents.

Favret-Saada (1980, 1989) argues that witchcraft beliefs and the ways Brocage families tried to divert witchcraft from themselves "worked" better as therapy and as a resolution for family problems than psychiatry did. In these ways the tensions generated inside families were diffused onto unspecified neighbours by the unwitcher.

More recently, La Fontaine (1992, 1997) suggests that, from an anthropological perspective, allegations about the sexual assault of children in rituals described as witchcraft or satanic worship in contemporary England can be seen as a modern day witch-hunt. The sexual assault of children exemplifies a major form of evil that is destructive of all order, and its perpetrators place themselves outside normal society or even humanity as a whole. Characteristically, the figure of the witch personifies such inhuman evil.

British child protection workers, therapists, and Christian fundamentalists made the allegations that, in secret gatherings, robed or masked people sexually abuse children in rituals that also include bestiality, forced abortions, animal and human sacrifices, and even acts of cannibalism. The founder of a British charity expressed the view that 4,000 children had been sacrificed in Great Britain alone.

Confessions of participation in witchcraft rituals and the rather incoherent accounts of survivors clothe the idea of witchcraft and devil worship with a unique air of realism. The fact that various forms of occultism do exist also supports modern allegations of satanism. The lack of corroborating evidence from police investigations and from the courts lends credence to thoughts about an international conspiracy and protection by important members of society.

La Fontaine argues that tensions arise from the perception that the fundamental assumption of parental altruism that underpins the concept of the family is being destroyed. In England the victims of child abuse come from unstable families in areas of long-term deprivation. They are marked by high unemployment, residence in run-down urban estates, histories of broken marital relations and police arrests, and considerable child neglect. Many children had suffered from delayed development or from emotional problems.

Conclusions

Witchcraft cannot simply be dismissed as a frill, on the edge of fantasy. Witchcraft relates to perennial problems of human existence such as misfortune, suffering, death, morality, desire, and inequalities in wealth and power. These problems of existence rank among the most compelling forces that motivate people to action. As Geschiere (1997) shows, the power of witchcraft beliefs derives precisely from their open-endedness and from their capacity to incorporate such multiple and diverse meanings. The indeterminancy of discourses allows for the constant integration of new themes and permits alternative interpretations that make witchcraft hard to refute. It is for these reasons that witchcraft exists in so many different times and places and that it deserves to be taken seriously by anthropologists.

References

Boyer P., and S. Nissenbaum. 1974. *Salem Possessed: The Social Origins of Witchcraft*. Cambridge, Mass.: Harvard University Press.

Cardozo, A. Rebecca. 1972. A modern American witch-craze. In *Witchcraft and Sorcery*, edited by Max Marwick. Harmondsworth: Penguin.

Ciekawy, Diane, and Peter Geschiere. 1998. Containing witchcraft: Conflicting scenarios in postcolonial Africa. *African Studies Review* 41 (3):1–14.

Comaroff, Jean, and John Comaroff. 1993. Introduction. In *Modernity and Its Malcontents: Ritual and Power in Post-colonial Africa*, edited by Jean Comaroff and John Comaroff. Chicago: University of Chicago Press.

Delamont, Sara. 1995. *Appetites and Identities: An Introduction to the Social Anthropology of Western Europe*. London: Routledge.

Evans-Pritchard, E. E. 1937. *Witchcraft, Oracles and Magic Amongst the Azande of Anglo-Egyptian Sudan*. Oxford: Oxford University Press.

Favret-Saada, J. 1980. *Deadly Words: Witchcraft in Brocage*. Cambridge: Cambridge University Press.

———. 1989. Unwitching as therapy. *American Ethnologist* 16 (1):40–56.

Fisiy, Cyprian F. 1998. Containing occult practices: Witchcraft trials in Cameroon. *African Studies Review* 41 (3): 143–164.

Fortune, Reo F. 1932. *Sorcerers of Dobu: The Social Anthropology of the Dobu Islands of the Western Pacific.* London: Routledge.

Geschiere, Peter. 1997. *The Modernity of Witchcraft: Politics of the Occult in Post-colonial Africa.* Charlottesville: University of Virginia Press.

Kelly, Raymond. 1976. Witchcraft and sexual relations: An exploration in the social and semantic implications of the structure of belief. In *Man and Woman in the New Guinea Highlands,* edited by P. Brown and G. Buchbinder. Washington, DC: AAA Special Publications No. 8, 36–53.

Kluckhohn, Clyde. 1944. *Navaho Witchcraft.* Boston: Beacon Press.

La Fontaine, Jean. 1992. Concepts of evil, witchcraft and the sexual abuse of children in modern England. *Etnofoor* 5 (1/2): 6–20.

———. 1997. *Speak of the Devil: Tales of Satanic Abuse in Contemporary England.* Cambridge: Cambridge University Press.

Lattas, Andrew. 1993. Sorcery and colonialism: Illness, dreams and death as political languages in West New Britain. *Man* (n.s.) 28 (2): 51–77.

Lawrence, D. L. 1982. Reconstructing the menstrual taboo. *Anthropological Quarterly* 55 (2): 94–98.

Marwick, Max. 1965. *Sorcery and Its Social Setting: A Study of the Northern Rhodesian Cewa.* Manchester: Manchester University Press.

Middleton, John, and E. Winter, eds. 1963. *Witchcraft and Sorcery in East Africa.* London: Routledge and Kegan Paul.

Parrinder, Geoffrey. 1963. *Witchcraft: European and African.* London: Faber and Faber.

Stephen, Michele. 1986. Introduction. In *Sorcerer and Witch in Melanesia,* edited by Michele Stephen. Carlton, Victoria: Melbourne University Press, 1–14.

Stewart, Charles. 1991. *Demons and the Devil.* Princeton, N.J.: Princeton University Press.

Thomas, Keith. 1971. *Religion and the Decline of Magic.* New York: Charles Scribner's Sons.

Turner, Victor. 1964. Witchcraft and sorcery: Taxonomy versus dynamics. *Africa* 34 (4): 314–325.

9

Language, Race, and White Public Space

Jane H. Hill

Jane Hill is Regents Professor and professor of anthropology with a joint appointment in linguistics, at the University of Arizona. She received her PhD from UCLA. She is a sociolinguist of Native American languages, and has worked with Tohono O'odham and Nahuatl speakers on issues of identity and self-construction. She has served as president of the American Anthropological Association.

The Study of Racism in Anthropology

Anthropologists share a contradictory heritage: Our intellectual ancestors include both founders of scientific racism and important pioneers of the antiracist movement. After many years in which anthropologists have given far less attention to racism as an object of cultural analysis than have many of

Reprinted from *American Anthropologist* 100, no. 3 (1998).

our sister disciplines, we are now returning to work that honors and advances our antiracist heritage.

Racism should be as central a question for research in cultural anthropology as "race" has been in biological anthropology. We have always been interested in forms of widely shared apparent irrationality, from divination to the formation of unilineal kin groups to the hyperconsumption of (or abstention from) the flesh of cattle, and racism is precisely this kind of phenomenon. Why, if nearly all scientists concur that human "races" are imaginary, do so many highly educated, cosmopolitan, economically secure people continue to think and act as racists? We know that "apparent irrationalities" seldom turn out to be the result of ignorance or confusion. Instead, they appear locally as quite rational, being rooted in history and tradition, functioning as important organizing principles in relatively enduring political ecologies, and lending coherence and meaning to complex and ambiguous human experiences. Racism is no different: As Smedley (1993:25) has argued, "race . . . [is] a worldview . . . a cosmological ordering system structured out of the political, economic, and social realities of peoples who had emerged as expansionist, conquering, dominating nations on a worldwide quest for wealth and power." Racism challenges the most advanced anthropological thinking, because racial formation processes (Omi and Winant 1994) are contested and contradictory, yet global in their scope. At the local level racial practices (Winant 1994) can be very complex. Yet emerging global "racialscapes" (Harrison 1995:49, borrowing from Appadurai 1990) encompass even the most remote populations, as when the Taiap of the backwaters of the Lower Sepik River feel themselves to be "Black" as against "White" (Kulick 1993).

From "All Languages are Equal" to the Study of Racializing Discourses

Like other anthropologists (and other linguists), linguistic anthropologists have made "education," with its implicit assumption of a confrontation with "ignorance," their central antiracist strategy. Attempts to inoculate students against beliefs in "primitive languages," "linguistic deprivation," or the idea that bilingualism (in certain languages) is inevitably seditious can be found in every introductory textbook in linguistics, and major scholars in the field have tried to spread the message not only as classroom educators, but as public intellectuals in a wide range of functions. And what have we to show for these efforts? "Official English" legislation on the books in many states, and, in the winter of 1996–97, a nationwide "moral panic" (Hall et al. 1978)[1] about whether "Ebonics" might be discussed in the classrooms of Oakland, California. In the case of the Ebonics panic, the nearly universal reaction

---

[1]Hall et al. (1978) borrow the notion of "moral panic" from Cohen (1972).

among linguists[2] and linguistic anthropologists was "We must redouble our efforts at education! How can we make classroom and textbook units on the equality of all languages, let alone all varieties of English, more effective? How can we place opinion pieces to fight this nonsense?" The problem here, of course, is that such interventions not only neglect the underlying cultural logic of the stigmatization of African American English, but also neglect the much deeper problem pointed out by James Baldwin: "It is not the Black child's language which is despised: It is his experience" (Baldwin 1979, cited in Lippi-Green 1997)—and Baldwin might have added, had he not been writing in the *New York Times*, "and his body."

Antiracist education in linguistics and linguistic anthropology has centered on demonstrations of the equality and adequacy of racialized forms of language, ranging from Boas's ([1889]1982) demolition of the concept of "alternating sound" and "primitive languages" to Labov's (1972) canonical essay on "The logic of non-standard English."[3] But until very recently, there has been little research on the "culture of language" of the dominant, "race-making" (Williams 1989) populations. New studies are beginning to appear, such as Fabian (1986), Silverstein (1987), Woolard (1989), and Lippi-Green (1997). Urciuoli's (1996) ethnography of speaking of Spanish and English among Puerto Ricans in New York City is perhaps the first monograph on the talk of a racialized population that foregrounds, and contributes to, contemporary theories of racial formation processes through her analysis of cultural phenomena such as "accent" and "good English."

A central theoretical commitment for many linguistic anthropologists, that "culture is localized in concrete, publicly accessible signs, the most important of which are actually occurring instances of discourse" (Urban 1991:1), prepares us to contribute in new ways to the untangling of the complexity of racism. Furthermore, such study is an obvious extension of an active line of research on linguistic ideologies (Woolard and Schieffelin 1994). We can explore questions like: What kinds of signs are made "concrete and publicly accessible" by racializing discourses? What kinds of discourses count, or do not count, as "racist," and by what (and whose) cultural logic? What are the different kinds of racializing discourses, and how are these distributed in speech communities? What discourse processes socialize children as racial subjects?[4] What are

[2]In a survey of 34 entries, encompassing about 100 messages, under the heading "Ebonics" on Linguist, the list that probably reaches the largest number of linguists, I found only one explicit mention of "racism" by an author who used the expression "institutional racism." It is, perhaps, appropriate for linguists to focus on their special areas of scholarly expertise, and it is certainly the case that there may be a linguistic dimension to the educational problems confronted by many African American children, but the neglect of racism on the list was quite striking. It was sometimes addressed obliquely and euphemistically, as with one author's proposal of the "special" situation of African Americans in the United States.

[3]The "all languages are equal" argument continues in spite of a warning by Dell Hymes (1973) that this claim is technically incorrect in many subtle ways.

[4]Hirschfeld (1996) documents the very early association between raced categories and an essentialized understanding of "human kinds" for young children in the United States.

the discourses of resistance, and what do they reveal about the forms of racism? What discourse processes relate the racialization of bodies to the racialization of kinds of speech? And all of these questions must, of course, be qualified by the question, in what kinds of contexts?

"Spanish Accents" and "Mock Spanish": Linguistic Order and Disorder in White Public Space

To illustrate a linguistic-anthropological approach to these issues, I build on an analysis by Urciuoli (1996), recentering it from her research on bilingual Puerto Ricans in New York City to a national community of Whites.[5] I have been looking at uses of Spanish by Whites, both through on-the-spot observation of informal talk and through following as wide a range as possible of media and sites of mass reproduction such as advertising fliers, gift coffee cups, souvenir placemats, and greeting cards, for several years. First, I review Urciuoli's analysis of the racialization of Puerto Ricans through attention to their linguistic "disorder."

Puerto Rican Linguistic Marginalization: Disorderly Order

Urciuoli argues that her consultants experience language as differentiated into two spheres. In an "inner sphere" of talk among intimates in the household and neighborhood, the boundaries between "Spanish" and "English" are blurred and ambiguous both formally and functionally. Here, speakers exploit linguistic resources with diverse histories with great skill and fluency, achieving extremely subtle interactional effects. But in an "outer sphere" of talk (and engagement with text) with strangers and, especially, with gatekeepers like court officers, social workers, and schoolteachers, the difference between Spanish and English is "sharply objectified" (Urciuoli 1996:2). Boundaries and order are everything. The pressure from interlocutors to keep the two languages "in order" is so severe that people who function as fluent bilinguals in the inner sphere become so anxious about their competence that sometimes they cannot speak at all. Among the most poignant of the intricate ambiguities of this duality are that worries about being "disorderly" are never completely absent

---

[5]I am mindful of Hartigan's (1997) argument that "Whites" are by no means a homogeneous population. Indeed, in other work (Hill 1995) I have suggested that working-class speakers are less likely to use "Mock Spanish" than are other Whites. Much of my material comes from mass media that are part of the homogenizing project of "whiteness," and there is no question that different "Whites" experience this project in different ways. I use "Whites" here (perhaps injudiciously) as a sort of shorthand required first by lack of space and second because the data required to precisely characterize the population I have in mind are not available. Certainly it includes White elites such as screenwriters and nationally syndicated columnists.

from the intimacies of the inner sphere, and people who successfully negotiate outersphere order are vulnerable to the accusation that they are "acting White," betraying their friends and relatives.

Urciuoli observes that a (carefully managed) Spanish is licensed in the outer sphere in such contexts as "folklife festivals," as part of processes of "ethnification" that work to make difference "cultural, neat, and safe" (Urciuoli 1996:9).[6] But Whites hear other public Spanish as impolite and even dangerous. Urciuoli (1996:35) reports that "nearly every Spanish-speaking bilingual I know . . . has experienced complaints about using Spanish in a public place." Even people who always speak English "in public" worry about their "accents." While "accent" is a cultural dimension of speech and therefore lives largely in the realm of the imaginary, this construct is to some degree anchored in a core of objective phonetic practices that are difficult to monitor, especially when people are nervous and frightened. Futhermore, it is well-known that Whites will hear "accent" even when, objectively, none is present, if they can detect any other signs of a racialized identity.[7] Speakers are anxious about far more than "accent," however: they worry about cursing, using vocabulary items that might seem uncultivated, and even about using too many tokens of "you know." Mediated by cultural notions of "correctness" and "good English," failures of linguistic order, real and imagined, become in the outer sphere signs of race: "difference as inherent, disorderly, and dangerous" (Urciuoli 1996:9).

The main point for my argument is that Puerto Ricans experience the "outer sphere" as an important site of their racialization, since they are always found wanting by this sphere's standards of linguistic orderliness. My research suggests that precisely the opposite is true for Whites. Whites permit themselves a considerable amount of disorder precisely at the language boundary that is a site of discipline for Puerto Ricans (and other members of historically Spanish-speaking populations in the United States)—that is, the boundary between Spanish and English in public discourse. I believe that this contrast, in which White uses of Spanish create a desirable "colloquial" presence for Whites, but uses of Spanish by Puerto Ricans (and members of other historically Spanish-speaking groups in the United States) are "disorderly and dangerous," is one of the ways in which this arena of usage is constituted as a

---

[6]Urciuoli (1996:16) points out that it is essential to use Spanish in the folklife festival context because to translate songs, the names of foods, and the like into English would render them less "authentic," this property being essential to claims on "ethnicity" that are one way to resist racialization.

[7]Here the canonical study is the matched-guise test conducted by Rubin (1992). Sixty-two undergraduate native speakers of English listened to a brief lecture (on either a science or humanities topic) recorded by a native speaker of English from central Ohio. While they listened, one group of students saw a slide of a White woman lecturer. The other half saw a slide of an Asian woman in the same setting and pose (and even of the same size, and with the same hair style, as the White woman). Students who heard the lecture under the "Asian slide" condition often reported that the lecturer had an Asian accent and, even more interestingly, scored lower on tests of comprehension of the lecture.

part of what Page and Thomas (1994) have called "White public space": a morally significant set of contexts that are the most important sites of the practices of racializing hegemony, in which Whites are invisibly normal, and in which racialized populations are visibly marginal and the objects of monitoring ranging from individual judgement to Official English legislation.

White Linguistic Normalcy: Orderly Disorder

While Puerto Ricans are extremely self-conscious about their "Spanish" accents in English, heavy English "accents" in Spanish are perfectly acceptable for Whites, even when Spanish speakers experience them as "like a fingernail on the blackboard." Lippi-Green (1997) points out the recent emergence of an industry of accent therapists, who offer their services to clients ranging from White southerners to Japanese executives working at American plant sites. But the most absurd accents are tolerated in Spanish, even in Spanish classes at the graduate level. I have played to a number of audiences a tape of a *Saturday Night Live* skit from several years ago, in which the actors, playing television news writers at a story conference, use absurdly exaggerated "Spanish" accents in names for Mexican food, places, sports teams, and the like. The Latino actor Jimmy Smits appears and urges them to use "normal anglicizations" (Hill 1993a). Academic audiences find the skit hilarious, and one of its points (it permits multiple interpretations) seems to be that it is somehow inappropriate for Whites to try to sound "Spanish."

While Puerto Ricans agonize over whether or not their English is cultivated enough, the public written use of Spanish by Whites is often grossly nonstandard and ungrammatical. Hill (1993a) includes examples ranging from street names, to advertising, to public-health messages. *Wash Your Hands/Lava sus manos*, originally reported by Peñalosa (1980) in San Bernardino County, California, can be found in restrooms all over the southwestern United States. Peñalosa observed that this example is especially remarkable since it has as many grammatical errors as it has words.[8] An excellent case was the reprinting by the *Arizona Daily Star* (August 10, 1997) of an essay by the Colombian Novelist Gabriel García Márquez that originally appeared in the *New York Times* (August 3, 1997). All of the diacritics on the Spanish words—and the problem of accent marks had been one of García Márquez's main points—were missing in the *Star* version. Tucson is the home of a major university and has a large Spanish-speaking population, and the audience for the piece (which appeared on the op-ed page of the Sunday edition) no doubt included many people who are literate in Spanish. Clearly, however, the *Star* was not concerned about offering this audience a literate text.

---

[8]It should be *Lavarse las manos*, the usual directive for public places being the infinitive (e.g., *No fumar* 'No Smoking,' *No estacionarse* 'No Parking'), the verb being reflexive, and body parts are not labeled by the possessive pronoun *su* unless they are detached from the body of their owner.

While Puerto Rican code switching is condemned as disorderly, Whites "mix" their English with Spanish in contexts ranging from coffee-shop chat to faculty meetings to the evening network newscasts and the editorial pages of major newspapers. Their "Mock Spanish"[9] incorporates Spanish-language materials into English in order to create a jocular or pejorative "key." The practices of Mock Spanish include, first, semantic pejoration of Spanish loans: the use of positive or neutral Spanish words in humorous or negative senses. Perhaps the most famous example is *macho*, which in everyday Spanish merely means "male." Equally important are Spanish expressions of leave-taking, like *adiós* and *hasta la vista,* used in Mock Spanish as kidding (or as serious) "kiss-offs" (Mock-Spanish "adios" is attested in this sense from the mid-nineteenth century). A second strategy borrows obscene or scatological Spanish words for use as Mock-Spanish euphemisms, as on the handwritten sign "Casa de Pee-Pee" on the door of the women's restroom in the X-ray department of a Tucson clinic, a coffee cup that I purchased in a gift shop near the University of Arizona Main Gate that bears the legend "Caca de Toro," and, of course, the case of *cojones,* exemplified below. In the third strategy, elements of "Spanish" morphology, mainly the suffix *-o,* often accompanied by "Spanish" modifiers like *mucho* or *el,* are borrowed to create jocular and pejorative forms like "el-cheap-o," "numero two-o," or "mucho trouble-o." In a recent example, heard on PBS's *Washington Week in Review,* moderator Ken Bode observed that, had the "palace coup" in the House of Representatives in July 1997 not been averted, the Speaker of the House Newt Gingrich would have been "Newt-o-Frito." The last major strategy of Mock Spanish is the use of "hyperanglicized" and parodic pronunciations and orthographic representations of Spanish loan words, as with "Grassyass," "Hasty lumbago," and "Fleas Navidad" (a picture of a scratching dog usually accompanies this one, which shows up every year on Christmas cards).

Mock Spanish is attested at least from the end of the eighteenth century, and in recent years it has become an important part of the "middling style" (Cmiel 1990), a form of public language that emerged in the nineteenth century as a way for elites to display democratic and egalitarian sensibilities by incorporating colloquial and even slangy speech. Recent relaxations of proscriptions against public vulgarity have made even quite offensive usages within Mock Spanish acceptable at the highest level of public discourse, as when the then-Ambassador to the United Nations Madeleine Albright addressed the Security Council after Cuban aircraft had shot down two spy planes manned by Cuban exiles: Cuban president Fidel Castro, she said, had shown "not *cojones,*

---

[9]In earlier publications (e.g., Hill 1993b), I referred to these practices as "Junk Spanish." I thank James Fernandez for the expression "Mock Spanish" and for convincing me that "Junk Spanish" was a bad nomenclatural idea, and the source of some of the problems I was having getting people to understand what I was working on (many people, including linguists and anthropologists, assumed that by "Junk Spanish" I meant something like the "Border Spanish" of native speakers of Spanish, rather than jocular and parodic uses of Spanish by English speakers). The most extensive discussion of Mock Spanish available is Hill (1995).

but cowardice." Although many Spanish speakers find this particular usage exceptionally offensive,[10] Albright's sally was quoted again and again in admiring biographical pieces in the major English-language news media after she was nominated to be Secretary of State (e.g., Gibbs 1996:33).

The Semiotics of Mock Spanish

In previous work (e.g., Hill 1995), I analyzed Mock Spanish as a "racist discourse." That is, I took its major functions to be the "elevation of whiteness" and the pejorative racialization of members of historically Spanish-speaking populations. Mock Spanish accomplishes the "elevation of whiteness" through what Ochs (1990) has called "direct indexicality": the production of nonreferential meanings or "indexes" that are understood and acknowledged by speakers. Speakers of Mock Spanish say that they use it because they have been exposed to Spanish—that is, they are cosmopolitan.[11] Or, that they use it in order to express their loyalty to, and affiliation with, the Southwest (or California or Florida)—that is, they have regional "authenticity." Or that they use it because it is funny—that is, they have a sense of humor. In one particular elaborate example, in the film *Terminator 2: Judgement Day,* Mock Spanish is used to turn Arnold Schwarzenegger, playing a cyborg, into a "real person," a sympathetic hero instead of a ruthless and terrifying machine. When Schwarzenegger, who has just returned from the future, answers a request with a curt Germanic "Affirmative," the young hero of the film, a 12-year-old White boy supposedly raised on the streets of Los Angeles, tells him, "No no no no no. You gotta listen to the way people talk!" He then proceeds to teach Schwarzenegger the Mock Spanish tags "No problemo" and "Hasta la vista, baby" as part of a register that also includes insults like "Dickwad."[12]

Analysis reveals that Mock Spanish projects, in addition to the directly indexed message that the speaker possesses a "congenial persona," another

---

[10]I am indebted to Professor Raúl Fernández of the University of California-Irvine for a copy of a letter he wrote to the *Los Angeles Times* protesting the appearance of *cojones* in a film review. Ernest Hemingway is probably to blame for the widespread knowledge of this word among monolingual speakers of English.

[11]While some Whites who use Mock Spanish have a classroom competence in that language (I was a case in point), most of the speakers I have queried say that they do not "speak Spanish."

[12]An anonymous referee for the *American Anthropologist* argues that this analysis, suggesting that the "elevation of whiteness" is accomplished through direct indexicality, it is not exactly correct. Instead, the direct indexicality of Mock Spanish elevates the individual, conveying "I am a nice/easy-going/funny/locally-rooted/ cosmopolitan person." The elevation of "whiteness" is then accomplished indirectly when combined with the indirectly indexed message "I am White." This is an interesting suggestion, but I think the *Terminator 2: Judgment Day* sequence argues that the indexicality is direct: Mock Spanish is precisely "the way people talk"—and "people" can only be that group that is unmarked and thereby "White." Thus positive individual qualities and "whiteness" are simultaneously indexed. (A direct version of this, perhaps mercifully obsolete, is the expression that applauds some act of good fellowship with "That's mighty White of you.")

set of messages: profoundly racist images of members of historically Spanish-speaking populations. These messages are the product of what Ochs (1990) calls "indirect indexicality" in that, unlike the positive direct indexes, they are never acknowledged by speakers. In my experience, Whites almost always deny that Mock Spanish could be in any way racist. Yet in order to "make sense of" Mock Spanish, interlocutors require access to very negative racializing representations of Chicanos or Latinos as stupid, politically corrupt, sexually loose, lazy, dirty, and disorderly. It is impossible to "get" Mock Spanish—to find these expressions funny or colloquial or even intelligible—unless one has access to these negative images. An exemplary case is a political cartoon in my collection, showing a picture of Ross Perot pointing to a chart that says, among other things, "Perot for El Presidente." This is funny only if the audience can juxtapose the pompous and absurd Perot with the negative image of a banana-republic dictator, dripping with undeserved medals. It is only possible to "get" "Hasta la vísta, baby" if one has access to a representation of Spanish speakers as treacherous. "Mañana" works as a humorous substitute for "later" only in conjunction with an image of Spanish speakers as lazy and procrastinating. My claim that Mock Spanish has a racializing function is supported by the fact that on humorous greeting cards (where it is fairly common) it is often accompanied by grossly racist pictorial representations of "Mexicans."

I have labeled Mock Spanish a "covert racist discourse" because it accomplishes racialization of its subordinate-group targets through indirect indexicality, messages that must be available for comprehension but are never acknowledged by speakers. In this it contrasts with "vulgar racist discourse," which uses the direct referential function in statements like, "Mexicans just don't know how to work," or hate speech ("Lazy greaser!"), which seems to operate through the performative function as a direct verbal "assault" (Matsuda et al. 1993). It is not exactly like the kind of kidding around that most Whites will admit can be interpreted as racist, as when David Letterman joked that the artificial fat olestra, which can cause abdominal pain and diarrhea, was "endorsed by the Mexican Health Department" (*New York Times*, August 24, 1997:F12). It also contrasts with the "elite racist discourse" identified by van Dijk (1993). Van Dijk pointed out that like Mock Spanish this type has as one function the presentation by the speaker of a desirable persona. Since "being racist" is an undesirable quality, tokens often begin with qualifications like "I'm not a racist, but . . ." and then continue with a racializing argument like "I really resent it that all these Mexicans come up here to have babies so that American taxpayers will support them." Such qualifications do not make sense with Mock Spanish: One cannot say, "I'm not a racist, but no problemo," or "I'm not a racist, but comprende?," or "I'm not a racist, but adios, sucker." The reason this frame does not work is because Mock Spanish racializes its objects only covertly, through indirect indexicality.

Mock Spanish sometimes is used to constitute hate speech (as in posters saying "Adios, Jose" held by demonstrators supporting anti-immigration laws in California), and co-occurs with racist joking and with vulgar and elite racist discourses as well. It is sometimes used to address apparent Spanish speakers; many of my consultants report being addressed as "amigo," and Vélez-Ibáñez (1996:86) reports an offensive use of "comprende?" (pronounced [kəmprɛndiy]). However, it is found very widely in everyday talk and text on topics that have nothing to do with race at all. Because of its covert and indirect properties, Mock Spanish may be an exceptionally powerful site for the reproduction of White racist attitudes. In order to be "one of the group" among other Whites, collusion in the production of Mock Spanish is frequently unavoidable.

In my previous work, reviewed above, I have assumed that the "elevation of whiteness" and the constitution of a valued White persona was accomplished in Mock Spanish entirely through direct indexicality. However, in the light of Urciuoli's new work on the imposition of "order" on Puerto Ricans, I now believe that Mock Spanish accomplishes the "elevation of whiteness" in two ways: first, through directly indexing valuable and congenial personal qualities of speakers, but, importantly, also by the same type of indirect indexicality that is the source of its negative and racializing messages. It is through indirect indexicality that using Mock Spanish constructs "White public space," an arena in which linguistic disorder on the part of Whites is rendered invisible and normative, while the linguistic behavior of members of historically Spanish-speaking populations is highly visible and the object of constant monitoring.

Research on "whiteness" (e.g., Frankenberg 1993) has shown that Whites practice not only the construction of the domain of "color" and the exclusion from resources of those racialized as "colored," but also the constitution of "whiteness" as an invisible and unmarked "norm."[13] Like all such norms, this one is built as bricolage, from the bits and pieces of history, but in a special way, as what Williams (1989), borrowing from Gramsci, calls a "transformist hegemony": "its construction results in a national process aimed at homogenizing heterogeneity fashioned around assimilating elements of heterogeneity through appropriations that devalue and deny their link to the marginalized others' contribution to the patrimony" (Williams 1989:435).[14]

Bits and pieces of language are important "elements of heterogeneity" in this work. Urciuoli (1996) has shown that precisely this kind of "heterogeneity"

---

[13]As Harrison (1995) points out, a more explicit construction of whiteness often appears among marginalized Whites, as in the current far-right "White pride" movement. She notes that this "undermines whatever incipient class consciousness exists among poor Whites" (Harrison 1995:63). Thus we can see such movements as part of the very large cultural formation wherein "race" may be the single most important organizer of relationships, determinant of identity, and mediator of meaning (Winant 1994).

[14]Williams focuses her analysis on the "national process," the creation of what she calls the race/class/nation conflation, but the construction of whiteness is probably a project of global scope, and in fact Mock Spanish seems to be widespread in the English-speaking world. Bertie, a character in the Barrytown novels (*The Commitments, The Snapper, The Van,* which depict life in working-class Dublin) by the Irish author Roddy Doyle, often uses Mock Spanish. For another example from outside the United States, I am indebted to Dick Bauman for a headline from the gardening section of a Glasgow newspaper, inviting the reader to "Hosta la vista, baby!" (that is, to plant members of the genus *Hosta* for their decorative foliage).

is not permitted to Puerto Ricans. What I have tried to show above is that linguistic heterogeneity and even explicit "disorder" is not only permitted to Whites, it is an essential element of a desirable White public persona. To be White is to collude in these practices, or to risk censure as "having no sense of humor" or being "politically correct." But White practice is invisible to the monitoring of linguistic disorder. It is not understood by Whites as disorder—after all, they are not, literally, "speaking Spanish" (and indeed the phenomena of public ungrammaticality, orthographical absurdity, and parodic mispronunciations of Spanish are evidence that they go to some lengths to distance themselves from such an interpretation of their behavior [Hill 1993a]). Instead, they are simply being "natural": funny, relaxed, colloquial, authentic.

I have collected some evidence that members of historically Spanish-speaking populations do not share Whites' understanding of Mock Spanish. For instance, the sociologist Clara Rodríguez (1997:78) reports that she was "puzzled . . . with regard to [the] relevance" of the Mock Spanish in *Terminator 2: Judgement Day*. Literate Spanish speakers in the United States are often committed linguistic purists, and Mock Spanish is offensive to them because it contains so many grammatical errors and because it sometimes uses rude words. They focus on this concern, but of course they have little power to change White usage.[15] It is clear that many Spanish speakers do hear the racist message of Mock Spanish. In an interview,[16] a Spanish-speaking Chicano high school counselor in Tucson said, "You know, I've noticed that most of the teachers never use any Spanish around here unless it's something negative." A Spanish-speaking Chicano businesswoman said, "When you first hear that stuff, you think, that's nice, they're trying, but then you hear more and more and you realize that there's something nasty underneath." In lecturing on Mock Spanish, I have found that Chicano and Latino people in my audiences strongly concur with the main outlines of my analysis, and often bring me additional examples. Chicano scholars, especially Fernando Peñalosa (cf. 1980), have long pointed out the racist implications of disorderly Spanish usage by Whites. Thus, for thoughtful Spanish speakers, the fact that disorderly Spanish and "Mock Spanish" constitute a "White public space" is not news. One of the dimensions of this space is that disorder on the part of Whites (including not only Mock Spanish, but also cursing and a variety of locutionary sins of the "you know" type) is largely invisible, while disorder on the part of racialized populations is hypervisable to the point of being the object of expensive political campaigns and nationwide "moral panics."

[15]I have discovered only one case of apparent concern about Spanish-speaking opinion in reference to the use of Spanish in mass media. Chon Noriega (1997:88) reports that when the film *Giant* was presented for review to the Production Code Administration in 1955, Geoffrey Shurlock, the head of the PCA, requested that the ungrammatical Spanish in the film (in which Spanish appears without subtitles) be corrected, apparently for fear of offending the government of Mexico, then seen as a "good neighbor."

[16]Dan Goldstein and I have begun a project of interviewing members of historically Spanish-speaking populations about Mock Spanish. We have compiled a scrapbook of examples, and subjects are audiotaped as they leaf through these and comment on them.

More Sources for Homogeneous Heterogeneity

The "incorporation"[17] of linguistic elements into the linguistic "homogeneous heterogeneity" of White public space draws on many sources. Perhaps the most important is what Smitherman (1994) calls the "crossover" of forms from African American English (AAE).[18] Gubar (1997) builds on the work of Morrison (1992) and others in a richly detailed study of very widespread and pervasive incorporative processes in the usage of White artists and writers. However, AAE and White English are so thoroughly entangled in the United States that crossover is extremely difficult to study. While obvious "wiggerisms" like "Word to your Mother"[19] or moth-eaten tokens of minstrelsy like "Sho' nuff, Mistah Bones" are easy to spot, many other usages are curiously indeterminate.[20] Even where an AAE source is recognizable to an etymologist, it is often impossible to know whether the usage indexes any "blackness" to its user or audience. One way of understanding this indeterminacy might be to see it as a triumph of White racial practice. New tokens of White "hipness," often retrievable as Black in origin only by the most dogged scholarship (although often visible to Blacks), are constantly created out of AAE materials.

An example of indeterminate crossover appeared in the "For Better or for Worse" comic strip published in the *Arizona Daily Star* (August 22, 1997). Two White Canadian lads discuss how Lawrence should deal with his partner's departure to study music in Paris. Bobby, who is straight, tries to reassure Lawrence, who is gay,[21] that falling in love is always worth it, even knowing the risk of loss. Lawrence jokes, "Let it be known that this speech comes from a guy who's in a 'happening' relationship." "Happening" in this sense comes from AAE "happenin," but it seems unlikely that here it is intended to convey anything more than the strip creator's alertness to "the speech of today's young

[17] I borrow this term from Raymond Williams (1977).

[18] I do not include "Vernacular" (many scholars refer to "African American Vernacular English" or AAVE), because AAE has a full range of register ranging from street argot through middle-class conversational usage to formal oratory and *belles lettres*. Scholars like Smitherman (1988) and Morgan (1994) have criticized sociolinguists for typifying AAE only through attestations of street registers.

[19] Smitherman (1994:237) defines *wigger* as "literally, a white NIGGER, an emerging positive term for White youth who identify with HIP HOP, RAP, and other aspects of African American Culture." She gives the proper form of the affirmation as "Word to the Mother," but I first heard it (from a young White woman) in the form given.

[20] In the lexicon of AAE provided by Smitherman (1994) I recognized many forms in my own usage that she does not mark as "crossovers" (to give only one example, "beauty shop" for a hair-and-nails salon was the only term I knew for such establishments as I was growing up, and it was universally used by my grandmothers, aunts, and mother, all White ladies who would never have dreamed of essaying any "Dis and Dat" [Gubar's (1996) term for the adoption of AAE forms by White writers]). My grandfather, an egregious racist who grew up in southeastern Missouri, was very fond of "copacetic," which Smitherman attributes to the speech of "older blacks" and does not recognize as ever having "crossed over."

[21] A number of U.S. newspapers refused to publish the series of episodes in which Lawrence mourns his partner's departure.

people" (although the quotation marks around the form do suggest that she regards this register as not part of her own repertoire). Yet similar usages can be highly salient for Blacks: Lippi-Green (1997:196) quotes an audience member on an episode of Oprah Winfrey: "This is a fact. White America use black dialect on commercials every day. Be observant, people. Don't let nobody tell you that you are ignorant and that you don't speak right. Be observant. They started off Channel 7 Eyewitness news a few years ago with one word: whashappenin. So what's happening, America?"

Now, contrast the episode of "For Better or for Worse" described above with another episode, published a couple of years ago. Here the young people are on a ski slope, and one boy, Gordon, "hits on" (I am sure Smitherman [1994] is correct that this is AAE, but in my own usage it feels merely slangy) a pretty girl with our now-familiar token, "What's happening?" She "puts him down" (probably also AAE, but not in Smitherman 1994)[22] with "With you? Nada." While probably few White readers of this strip sense "blackness" in "What's happening?", most will immediately detect "Nada" as "Spanish." That is, while the "Black" indexicality of "What's happening" is easily suppressed, it is virtually impossible to suppress the "Spanish" indexicality of "Nada," which has in "Mock Spanish" the semantically pejorated sense "absolutely nothing, less than zero." It seems likely that there are tokens that originate in Mock Spanish where the original indexicality is suppressable (the word *peon*, pronounced [piyan], which appeared in English by the seventeenth century, may be an example of this type), but in general tokens of this practice are relatively easy to spot and interpret.

Because of this relative transparency of Mock Spanish, it is a good choice for linguistic-anthropological research. However, precisely because it is narrower in its range of opacity and transparency than is AAE "crossover," it must function somewhat differently in White public space, an issue that needs investigation. Furthermore, African Americans themselves apparently use Mock Spanish; Terry McMillan's novel, *How Stella Got Her Groove Back,* is rich in attestations in the speech of Stella, a beautiful and successful African American professional woman from California. In contrast, as far as I know no members of historically Spanish-speaking populations use Mock Spanish, at least not in anything like the routine way that Whites do.[23]

The same question, of different functions of such linguistic incorporations into White "homogeneous heterogeneity," occurs with borrowings from other languages. For instance, tokens of "mock French" like "Mercy buckets" and "bow-koo" do occur, but they are relatively rare, especially in comparison with the very

---

[22]The *American Heritage Dictionary of the English Language* (Third Edition) lists "put down" as "slang." Unsurprisingly, their sentence of attestation comes from the work of Dr. Alvin Pous-saint, an African American.

[23]Some Spanish speakers find some of the greeting cards in my sample funny. One woman said that she might send a "Moochos Smoochos" card (illustrating hyperanglicized parody and the use of Spanish morphology to be funny) to her husband; she said, "That one's kinda cute."

extensive use of French in advertising, especially in the fashion industry, to convey luxury and exclusivity. "Mock Italian" seems to have been relatively important in the 1940s and 1950s but is apparently on the way out; I have found very few examples of it. "Mock Yiddish" is common but is used by members of historically Yiddish-speaking groups as well as by outsiders. "Mock Japanese" "sayonara" is perfectly parallel to Mock Spanish "adios," but may be the only widely used token of this type.[24] In summary, "Mock" forms vary widely in relative productivity and in the kinds of contexts in which they appear. By far the richest examples of linguistic incorporations are Mock Spanish and AAE crossover.

Can Mock Forms Subvert the Order of Racial Practices?

A number of authors, including Hewitt (1986), Gubar (1997) and Butler (1997), have argued that usages that in some contexts are grossly racist seem to contain an important parodic potential that can be turned to the antiracist deconstruction of racist categorical essentializing. Hewitt studied Black-White friendships among young teenagers in south London and found a "productive dialogue of youth" (1986:99) in which he identifies antiracist potential. Especially notable were occasions where Black children would tease White friends as "nigger," and the White teens would reply with "honky" or "snowflake." Hewitt comments, "This practice . . . turns racism into a kind of effigy, to be burned up in an interactive ritual which seeks to acknowledge and deal with its undeniable presence whilst acting out the negation of its effects" (1986:238). Gubar (1997) suggests that posters by the artist Iké Udé (such as a famous image of Marilyn Monroe, but in "blackface," and a transformation of Robert Mapplethorpe's infamous "Man in a Polyester Suit" with white skin and a circumcised penis) may use the symbolic repertoire of racism as "crucial aesthetic means of comprehending racial distinction without entrenching or denying it" (Gubar 1997:256). An example in the case of Spanish might be the performance art of Guillermo Gómez Peña,[25] who creates frenzied mixtures of English and multiple registers and dialects of Spanish (and even Nahuatl). Butler (1997), writing in opposition to the proscription of the racist vocabulary by anti-hate speech legislation, argues that gays and lesbians have been able to subvert the power of "queer," and that other "hate words" may have similar potential. The kinds of

---

[24]"Honcho," from Japanese *han* "Squad" and *cho* "chief" (*American Heritage Dictionary of the English Language*, Third Edition) seems to be etymologically inaccessible as Japanese except to specialists; many Whites probably think that it is Spanish.

[25]See, for instance, his *Warrior for Gringostroika* (1991). However, Gómez Peña uses so much Spanish that one must be bilingual to understand him; his art seems to be addressed mainly to multilingual Spanish-speaking audiences. Woolard's (1988) study of a comic in 1970s Barcelona, who entertained audiences with jokes that code switched between Castilian and Catalan during a period of extreme linguistic conflict and purism, provides another example of this type of subversion.

games reported by Hewitt, however, remain reserved to childhood, unable to break through the dominant voices of racism; Hewitt found the kind of interracial friendship that permitted teasing with racist epithets essentially vanished from the lives of his subjects by the time they reached the age of 16. In the light of the analysis that I have suggested above, the "subversions" noted by Gubar and Butler can also be seen simply as one more example of "orderly" disorder that is reserved to elites in White public space, rather than as carnivalesque inversions. Or, perhaps we should say that carnivalesque inversions can be a "weapon of the strong" as well as a "weapon of the weak."[26] The art of a Gómez Peña, to the degree that it is acceptable to White audiences, may precisely "whiten" this performer and others like him.

An important possible exception is the phenomenon of "crossing," discussed by British sociolinguist Ben Rampton (1995), who reports extensive use of out-group linguistic tokens among British adolescents of a variety of ethnic origins, including strongly racialized populations like West Indians and South Asians as well as Whites. "Crossings," while they retain some potential to give offense, often seem simply to acknowledge what is useful and desirable in the space of urban diversity. Thus, working-class White girls learn the Panjabi lyrics to "bhangra" songs, and Bengali kids speak Jamaican creole (which seems to have emerged in general as a prestigious language among British youth, parallel to the transracial "hip-hop" phenomenon in the United States). Early reports by Shirley Brice Heath of new work with American adolescents has identified similar "crossing" phenomena.[27] However, only slightly more than a decade ago Hewitt (1986) found that such crossings did not survive the adolescent years. We cannot be sure that these phenomena are genuinely outside the linguistic order of racism until we understand dimensions of that order—within which age-graded cohorts may have a relatively enduring place. I have tried above to show how linguistic-anthropological attention to the history, forms, and uses of White language mixing can help us toward such an understanding.

Notes

Acknowledgments. I would especially like to thank María Rodríguez, Bambi Schieffelin, and Kathryn Woolard, who have provided me with valuable material on Mock Spanish.

[26]"Weapon of the weak" comes, of course, from Scott (1985). Work on discourses of resistance by scholars like Scott (see also 1990) and Bhabha (1994) often seems to imply that parody and humor are primarily strategies of resistance. However, it is obvious that humor is an important part of racist discourse, and the accusation that antiracists "have no sense of humor" is an important weapon of racists.

[27]In a colloquialism presented to the Department of Anthropology, University of Arizona, Tucson, January 27, 1997.

References Cited

Appadurai, Arjun. 1990. Disjuncture and Difference in the Global Cultural Economy. Public Culture 2:1–24.

Bhabha, Homi K. 1994. The Location of Culture. New York: Routledge.

Boas, Franz. [1889]1982. On Alternating Sounds. *In* The Shaping of American Anthropology, 1883–1911: A Franz Boas Reader. George W. Stocking, ed. Pp. 72–76. Chicago: University of Chicago Press.

Butler, Judith. 1997. Excitable Speech. New York: Routledge.

Cmiel, Kenneth. 1990. Democratic Eloquence. New York: William Morrow.

Cohen, Stan. 1972. Folk Devils and Moral Panics: The Creation of the Mods and the Rockers. London: MacGibbon and Kee.

Fabian, Johannes. 1986. Language and Colonial Power: The Appropriation of Swahili in the Former Belgian Congo, 1880–1938. Cambridge: Cambridge University Press.

Frankenberg, Ruth. 1993. White Women, Race Matters: The Social Construction of Whiteness. Minneapolis: University of Minnesota Press.

Gibbs, Nancy. 1996. An American Voice. Time 149(1):32–33.

Gómez-Peña, Guillermo. 1993. Warrior for Gringostroika. St. Paul, MN: Graywolf Press.

Gubar, Susan. 1997. Racechanges: White Skins, Black Face in American Culture. Oxford University Press.

Hall, Stuart, Chas Critcher, Tony Jefferson, John Clarke, and Brian Roberts. 1978. Policing the Crisis. London: The Macmillan Press Ltd.

Harrison, Faye V. 1995. The Persistent Power of "Race" in the Cultural and Political Economy of Racism. Annual Review of Anthropology 24:47–74.

Hartigan, John, Jr. 1997. Establishing the Fact of Whiteness. American Anthropologist 99:495–505.

Hewitt, Roger. 1986. White Talk Black Talk, Inter-Racial Friendship and Communication among Adolescents. Cambridge: Cambridge University Press.

Hill, Jane H. 1993a. Hasta La Vista, Baby: Anglo Spanish in the American Southwest. Critique of Anthropology 13:145–176.

———. 1993b. Is it Really "No Problemo"? *In* SALSA I: Proceedings of the First Annual Symposium about Language and Society—Austin. Robin Queen and Rusty Barrett, eds. Texas Linguistic Forum 33:1–12.

———. 1995. Mock Spanish: A Site for the Indexical Reproduction of Racism in American English. Electronic document. University of Chicago Langcult Site. http://www.cs.uchicago.edu/discussions/1-c.

Hirschfeld, Lawrence A. 1996. Race in the Making. Cambridge, MA: MIT Press/Bradford Books.

Hymes, Dell H. 1973. Language and Speech: On the Origins and Foundations of Inequality among Speakers. *In* Language as a Human Problem. Einar Haugen and Morton Bloomfield, eds. Pp. 45–72. New York: W. W. Norton and Co.

Kulick, Don. 1993. Language Shift and Cultural Reproduction. Cambridge: Cambridge University Press.

Labov, William. 1972. Language in the Inner City. Philadelphia: University of Pennsylvania Press.

Lippi-Green, Rosina. 1997. English with an Accent: Language, Ideology, and Discrimination in the United States. London: Routledge.

Matsuda, Mari J., Charles R. Lawrence III, Richard Delgado, and Kimberlé Williams Crenshaw, eds. 1993. Words that Wound: Critical Race Theory, Assaultive Speech, and the First Amendment. Boulder, CO: Westview Press.

McMillan, Terry. 1996. How Stella Got Her Groove Back. New York: Viking.

Morgan, Marcyliena. 1994. The African-American Speech Community: Reality and Sociolinguists. In Language and the Social Construction of Identity in Creole Situations. Marcyliena Morgan, ed. Pp. 121–150. Los Angeles: UCLA Center for Afro-American Studies.

Morrison, Toni. 1992. Playing in the Dark: Witness and the Literary Imagination. Cambridge, MA: Harvard University Press.

Noriega, Chon. 1997. Citizen Chicano: The Trials and Titillations of Ethnicity in the American Cinema, 1935–1962. In Latin Looks. Clara E. Rodríguez, ed. Pp. 85–103. Boulder, CO: Westview.

Ochs, Elinor. 1990. Indexicality and Socialization. In Cultural Psychology. James Stigler, Richard A. Shweder, and Gilbert Herdt, eds. Pp. 287–308. Cambridge: Cambridge University Press.

Omi, Michael, and Howard Winant. 1994. Racial Formation in the United States. 2nd edition. New York: Routledge.

Page, Helán E., and Brooke Thomas. 1994. White Public Space and the Construction of White Privilege in U.S. Health Care: Fresh Concepts and a New Model of Analysis. Medical Anthropology Quarterly 8:109–116.

Peñalosa, Fernando. 1980. Chicano Sociolinguistics. Rowley, MA: Newbury House Press.

Rampton, Ben. 1995. Crossing: Language and Ethnicity among Adolescents. London: Longman.

Rodríguez, Clara E. 1997. The Silver Screen: Stories and Stereotypes. In Latin Looks. Clara E. Rodríguez, ed. Pp. 73–79. Boulder, CO: Westview Press.

Rubin, D. L. 1992. Nonlanguage Factors Affecting Undergraduates' Judgments of Nonnative English-Speaking Teaching Assistants. Research in Higher Education 33:511–531.

Scott, James C. 1985. Weapons of the Weak: Everyday Forms of Peasant Resistance. New Haven, CT: Yale University Press.

———. 1990. Domination and the Arts of Resistance: Hidden Transcripts. New Haven CT: Yale University Press.

Silverstein, Michael. 1987. Monoglot "Standard" in America. Working Papers of the Center for Psychosocial Studies, 13. Chicago: Center for Psychosocial Studies.

Smedley, Audrey. 1993. Race in North America: Origin and Evolution of a Worldview. Boulder, CO: Westview Press.

Smitherman, Geneva. 1994. Black Talk: Words and Phrases from the Hood to the Amen Corner. Boston: Houghton Mifflin Company.

Smitherman-Donaldson, Geneva. 1988. Discriminatory Discourse on Afro-American Speech. *In* Discourse and Discrimination. Geneva Smitherman-Donaldson and Teun van Dijk, eds. Pp. 144–175. Detroit: Wayne State University Press.

Urban, Greg. 1991. A Discourse-Centered Approach to Culture. Austin: University of Texas Press.

Urciuoli, Bonnie. 1996. Exposing Prejudice: Puerto Rican Experiences of Language, Race, and Class. Boulder, CO: Westview Press.

Van Dijk, Teun A. 1993. Elite Discourse and Racism. Newbury Park, CA: Sage Publications.

Vélex-Ibáñez, Carlos G. 1996. Border Visions: Mexican Cultures of the Southwest United States. Tucson: University of Arizona Press.

Williams, Brackette. 1989. A Class Act: Anthropology and the Race to Nation across Ethnic Terrain. Annual Review of Anthropology 18:401–444.

Williams, Raymond. 1977. Marxism and Literature. Oxford University Press.

Winant, Howard. 1994. Racial Conditions: Politics, Theory, Comparisons. Minneapolis: University of Minnesota Press.

Woolard, Kathryn A. 1988. Codeswitching and Comedy in Catalonia. *In* Codeswitching: Anthropological and Sociolinguistic Perspectives. Monica Heller, ed. Pp. 53–70. Berlin: Mouton de Gruyter.

———. 1989. Sentences in the Language Prison. American Ethnologist 16:268–278.

Woolard, Kathryn A., and Bambi Schieffelin. 1994. Language Ideology. Annual Review of Anthropology 23:55–82.

10

"Ladies" behind Bars

A Liminal Gender as Cultural Mirror

John M. Coggeshall

John M. Coggeshall, an assistant professor of anthropology at Clemson University in South Carolina, has carried out fieldwork in two medium-security prisons in Illinois. He received his Ph.D. in 1984 from Southern Illinois University.

"You here to see the show?" the inmate leered. The focus of attention was the tall blond then receiving her food in the prison cafeteria. The workers filled her plate with polite deference, and as she walked between the tables her fine blond hair bounced over her shoulders. "Make you want to leave home?" the guard next to me teased. His joke clarified the significance of the episode I had just witnessed. The object of attention was genetically a male, reconstructed as female according to the perception of gender within the cultural rule system of prison. Behind bars, certain males become redefined as "ladies." I have not been able to discern any correlation between assigned gender and the type of crime

Reprinted from *Anthropology Today* 4, no. 4 (1988), Royal Anthropological Institute.

for which an inmate was sentenced. The process by which this transformation occurs reveals not only clues about gender construction in prison culture, but also suggests perceptions of gender identity in American culture in general.

Prison culture involves one predominant theme: control. To establish identity, males profess a culturally defined image to defend themselves from oppression by guards and other inmates. Men define themselves as males by juxtaposing maleness with femaleness, fabricating gender identity from the reflection. For inmates, the concept of female emerges from the concept of male. To borrow a well-known metaphor, the rib for Eve's creation is taken from Adam's side, and draws both its cultural significance and social status from the extraction. Woman is defined in contrast to man, and takes a lesser place at his side. In prison, males create females in their image, and by doing so, dominate and subjugate them.

The fieldwork upon which this study is based was conducted in two medium-security prisons in southern Illinois between 1984 and 1986. Within that time span I taught three university-level courses to about thirty adult inmates, constituting a range of racial group and criminal record diversity representative of the overall prison population. Their perceptions provided a portion of the field data, supplemented by my observations of and conversations with guards and staff. After having received some instruction on ethnographic data collection, a former student and then resident inmate, Gene Luetkemeyer, volunteered to collect additional information on "ladies" behind bars. His nine detailed interviews of various categories of inmates, identified in the text by pseudonyms, significantly enhanced the scope and detail of the study.

Prison culture is extremely complex, and deserves much more detailed study by anthropologists (see for example the treatment by Goffman 1961, Davidson 1983, and Cardozo-Freeman 1984).[1] Even my relatively brief "incarceration" has suggested numerous leads for future research. Gender identity in prison could be explored in much greater detail, describing for example the abusive context whereby young males might become pawns by an administration concerned with pacifying gangs. Another productive line of inquiry might explore the overall cultural context of gender identity in prison culture, for themes of sexuality pervade prison, indicating its cultural significance for staff as well as inmates.

Gender Perceptions of Convicts

Here the research concentrates on the gender perceptions of convicts, i.e., the long-term residents (Davidson 1983). Convict attitudes toward homosexual behaviour vary considerably from one individual to the next. Not all participate, and not all do so with the same self-perception or with the same purposes. A subtle distinction is made by many inmates between individuals who engage entirely

---

[1]In my other writings I have discussed various ways in which inmates successfully retaliate to maintain a sense of identity. Much more could be explored, but space constrains discussion.

in submissive, recipient homosexual intercourse, and those who participate in mutual exchange of pleasure. Further distinctions also exist. Certain types or categories of homosexuals, some of which are discussed below, provide a ranking of these attitudes. Despite intra-cultural variation, widespread agreement prevails on cultural definitions of masculine and feminine gender identities.

Inmates have provided various estimates for the amount of homosexual activity in prison.[2] All agree that long-timers are more likely to engage in such practices, for they have less of a future to anticipate, more opportunities for sexual pleasure to utilize, and relatively lenient punishments for violations. For example, Paul and Sandy, homosexual lovers, and Frank, Paul's straight friend, believe that about 65% of their prison population engages in homosexual activity, an estimate supported by Dr. B, an incarcerated medical doctor. While such numbers reveal the amount of control and coercion in prisoner culture, they also reveal the "need for love, affection, [and] intimate relationships" denied by the system, another inmate observes. Some ties are based on affection, but these are relatively rare.[3] Homosexual behaviour fulfills numerous functions in the social and cultural system of prison. Thus most inmates see it as at worst a repugnant necessity and at best a tolerable alternative.

Despite varying views on prevalence, prisoners agree on the general gender constructs in prisoner culture. Males in prison adopt a "masculine role," inmates assert. Robert describes "a big . . . macho weight-lifting virile Tom Selleck type guy" as typical of the stereotype. Weight lifters, in fact, seem to predominate in the category, for strength suggests masculinity. Real men vigorously protest sexual advances from other males by exhibiting a willingness to fight. Men are also seen as preoccupied with sexual gratification, and will obtain it at all costs.

Real men in prison are perceived as those who can keep, satisfy, and protect "women." The dominant sex partner is termed a "daddy," who watches out for and protects his "kid" or "girl." For some men, the acquisition of sex partners strongly resembles courting, where the pursuer flirts with and purchases commissary (snack foods, cosmetics, and similar items) for the object of his interest. Others acquire submissive sex partners by force. Ultimately, with either type, sexual partnerships are based on power and control, the complete domination of one person and one gender by another. In fact, domination defines the structure of the relationship which distinguishes the genders in prison.

However, in prison, since the culturally defined females had been males at one time, this presents "real" men with a gender identity problem: reconciling

[2]There are obvious implications for study of the spread of the AIDS virus. From my research it seems that most inmates had not yet thought about acquiring AIDS, probably on account of a low self-concept paralleling that of intravenous drug users. Since homosexual behaviour in prison cannot be eliminated, education and protection should be stressed.

[3]I do not mean to suggest that homosexual relationships in society at large are similar. In this article, I do not deal with homosexuality outside of prison, nor with affectional homosexuality inside prison, which does exist.

having sexual intercourse with males while maintaining a masculine self-concept. This adjustment is accomplished by means of a unique folk explanation of the origins of gender development and orientation. Basically, males in prison redefine selected males as females.

In direct contrast to these self-perceptions of males, men portray women in a painting of their own creation. Males see females as passive, subordinate, sexual objects. According to Robert, women are "sweet and charming," "fluid of movement," with "seductive gestures." Dr. B believes that he himself exhibits such effeminate qualities as "mild manners" and a "passive demeanour." Women are also viewed as attractive, and they use that allure to their advantage by feigning helplessness; this allows women to maintain a "certain power" over men, Paul feels. A woman might "use her charms" to "get what she wanted," while at the same time she might not "put out" sexually, according to Dr. B. Women often tease to coerce men, and sometimes withhold what had apparently been promised, he adds.

Of course, nearly all female staff in prison culture do not meet these stereotypes. By inmate definition, then, they must not be women. Such "non-women" do not challenge gender constructs but reinforce them further. Female guards and staff occupy positions of power and authority over inmates, decidedly atypical for women from a prisoner's perspective. Moreover, most of these women dress in ways to deliberately deaccentuate anatomical differences and to resemble their male counterparts uniformly. Because these women dress as "non-women" and control men, they cannot be women and must therefore be homosexuals or "dykes," as the convicts term them. To inmates, this can be the only explanation for women who do not act like women. Cultural reality persists as potentially disruptive anomalies disappear through redefinition.

Trapped Between Male and Female Roles

The process by which certain males become redefined as females in prison provides an example of Victor Turner's (1969) concept of liminality. Prisoner culture perceives certain males as being trapped in between male and female, thus necessitating the release of their true gender identities. The period of incarceration provides the "time out of time" necessary for the transfiguration to occur. In fact, inmate terms for the metamorphosis reveal this gender ambiguity: males "turn out" these non-males, transforming them into the cultural equivalent of females. The liminal gender is actually "male as female," betwixt and between both. Such individuals figuratively "turn out" to be females, reconstructed according to the prisoner cultural stereotypes of "female." They thus become their "true" selves at last.

This duality creates additional complications in self-identity for such men. Goffman (1961) noted the struggle inmates have in reconciling the staff's perception of them with their own self-concept. Inmates readjusting a sexual orientation share a similar problem. Dr. B explains that individuals who make the transition from male to female must reconcile past heterosexual behaviour with their present homosexual identity. The homosexual in prison must convince herself that this new self-perception had been her true identity all along. Thus she now has adapted the normal role befitting her identity and gender adjustment.

Vindication for the transformation comes as those forced to become homosexuals remain as such. The acceptance by the homosexual of her new gender identity and associated behaviour justifies the conversion in the eyes of the rest of the prison population. If the "male becoming female" had no natural proclivity or had not been submissive by nature and thus also female, she would never have agreed to have adopted a feminine identity. As Frank (an inmate) explains, those who surrender are weak, and females are weak. Therefore those who surrender must be female by nature.

Folk conceptions of the origins of gender further support this perspective. Tommy (another inmate) notes that all humans are "conceived as female, then either, as foetuses, develop genitalia or not." Some individuals perpetuate, even unconsciously, this dualistic foetal identity into adulthood: they can be transformed or "turned out." Not resisting, or not resisting aggressively enough, merely validates this gender liminality. In a sense, it is only appropriate that those trapped betwixt and between be released, to unfetter their true natures. Even coercive gender conversion restores the natural order.

Prisoner culture divides homosexuals into several types, each defined on the basis of degree of sexual promiscuity, amount of self-conceptual pride, and severity of coercion used to turn them out. Generally, status declines as sexual promiscuity increases, self-concept decreases, and the types and intensity of coercion used in the conversion process increase.

The highest status category of homosexuals in prison is that of "queens" or "ladies," those who had come out both voluntarily and willingly. Prisoner cultural belief suggests that these individuals had been homosexual on the outside but may have lacked the freedom to have been themselves. Prison has provided them with a treasured opportunity to "come out," and they have accepted the freedom gratefully. Such individuals maintain a high status by remaining in control of their own lives and of their own self-concept.

Other individuals volunteer to be females, transforming themselves in order to acquire material comforts or social prestige. Terms for this general category vary, depending on the amount of coercion or force needed to "turn out" the female image. "Kids," "gumps," or "punks" describe individuals who in effect have sold their male identities, surrendering their culturally defined masculinity to be redefined as females.

Many other inmates, however, are forced to become homosexuals against their initial will. According to Wadley (another inmate): "[E]veryone is tested. The weak—of personality, personal power, willingness to fight, physical frailty, timidity—are especially susceptible. . . . Respect is given to one who can control the life of another," he adds. Those unwilling or unable to control others are thus themselves controlled. According to the cultural rules of gender identity in prison, those who dominate, by natural right, are males, and those who submit, by natural temperament, are females.

A Forced Female Role

Individuals forced to adopt a female role have the lowest status, and are termed "girls," "kids," "gumps," or "punks." Kids are kept in servitude by others, as a sign of the owner's power and prestige. Gumps are generally owned or kept by a gang, which collects money by prostituting the sexual favours of the unfortunate inmate. A gump may at one time have volunteered to come out to her feminine identity, but due to lack of personal status or power she has been forced to become sexually promiscuous for money or her physical survival. A punk, most agree, initially hesitates, and is turned out by coercion.

However transformed, most homosexuals in prison take on a feminine persona and appearance, even assuming a feminine name and requesting feminine pronouns as referents. The external transformation from male to female often is remarkable. Despite the formal restrictions of a dress code in prison, clothing styles may be manipulated rather patently to proclaim gender identity. Hair is often styled or curled and worn long. Even cosmetics are possible: black felt-tip pens provide eye liner and shadow; kool-aid substitutes for blush; and baby powder disguises prominent cheekbones. The personal appearance of homosexuals enhances their identity by demarcating them as obviously different from men.

Homosexuals perform numerous functions depending upon their status and relative freedom. Generally, the higher the status the more control one has over one's activities and one's life. High-status individuals such as Sandy select their own lovers. These couples live as husbands and wives, with the "little woman" providing domestic services such as laundry, cell cleaning, grooming, and sex.

Those with less status perform much the same tasks, but less voluntarily and with less consideration from their daddies. Once an inmate has been forced to adopt a submissive lifestyle, the nightmare of domination becomes more intense. For example, gumps might be forced to pleasure a gang chief, or may be passed down to soldiers in the gang for enjoyment. A particularly attractive kid might be put "on the stroll," forced to be a prostitute, for the financial benefit of the gang. Business may prove to be so lucrative that some homosexuals must seek protective custody (solitary confinement) to get some rest.

According to Dr. B, some homosexuals actually prefer to be dominated. The prevalent value system in prison suggests that those "females" who resist sexual attacks vicariously enjoy being dominated physically and sexually by more powerful individuals.

Hated and abused, desired and adored, ladies in prison occupy an important niche: they are the women of that society, constructed as such by the male-based perception of gender identity. In prison, females are termed "holes" and "bitches," reflecting the contempt which Dr. B believes to be characteristic of society's view of lower-class women in general. In prison, he adds, a homosexual "is likely to receive much of the contempt [and] pent-up hostility that would otherwise be directed at women." Herein lies the key to unlocking the deeper significance of gender construction in prisoner culture.

Gender Construction in Prison

Recall the general inmate perception of this liminal gender in prisoner culture. Homosexuals are owned and protected by daddies, who provide for their material and social comfort. In exchange, they provide sexual gratification. They often sell themselves and their bodies for material objects, promiscuously using their allure to manipulate men and to improve their social status. They feign helplessness in order to control their men. Ladies are emotional, helpless, and timid, while at the same time petulant, sassy, and demanding, nagging their men for attention. Best suited for certain tasks, homosexuals provide domestic and personal services for their daddies, serving their every whim.

Most fundamentally, homosexuals are sexual objects, to be used, abused, and discarded whenever necessary. Passive recipients of male power, they even enjoy being dominated and controlled. Males do them favours by releasing their "true" female identities through rape. In prison, sexuality equals power. Males have power, females do not, and thus males dominate and exploit the "weaker sex."

Ultimately, in whose image and likeness are these "males as females" created? Genetically female staff and administrators do not fit the stereotypical view, and thus provide no role models for ladies in prison. Males themselves draft the image of female in prison, forming her from their own perceptions. Males "turned out" as females perform the cultural role allotted to them by males, a role of submission and passivity. In actuality, males produce, direct, cast, and write the script for the cultural performance of gender identity behind bars.

In prison, woman is made in contrast to the image and likeness of man. Men define women as "not men," establishing their own self-identity from the juxtapositioning. Gender as a cultural construct is reflexive; each pole draws meaning from a negation of the other. As in Monteros (Brandes 1980), folk concepts reinforce the differences, emphasizing maleness at the expense of femaleness and the powerful at the expense of the powerless. By means of sexual domination, women remain in a culturally defined place of servitude and submission.

Prison Culture as a Distorting Mirror

It is precisely this concept of gender identity that has proven most disquieting about the status of homosexuals in prison. Granted, prison culture fosters a terribly distorted view of American culture.[4] Nevertheless, one sees a shadowy reflection in the mirror of prisoner culture which remains hauntingly familiar. As ladies are viewed by males in prison culture, so are females perceived by many males in American culture. Gender roles and attitudes in prison do not contradict American male values; they merely exaggerate the domination and exploitation already present. In prison gender constructs, one sees not contrasts but caricatures of gender concepts "on the street." Thus, the liminal gender of ladies behind bars presents, in reality, a cultural mirror grotesquely reflecting the predominant sexism of American society in general, despite initiatives by women to redefine their position and change gender relationships.

References

Brandes, Stanley. 1980. *Metaphors of Masculinity: Sex and Status in Andalusian Folklore.* Publications of the American Folklore Society (n.s.) Vol. 1. Philadelphia: University of Pennsylvania Press.

Cardoza-Freeman, Inez. 1984. *The Joint: Language and Culture in a Maximum-Security Prison.* Springfield, IL: Thomas.

Davidson, R. Theodore. 1983. *Chicano Prisoners: The Key to San Quentin.* Prospect Heights, IL: Waveland Press.

Goffman, Erving. 1961. *Asylums: Essays on the Social Situation of Mental Patients and Other Inmates.* Garden City, NY: Anchor Books.

Turner, Victor. 1969. *The Ritual Process.* Chicago: Aldine.

[4]Racial distinctions become exaggerated in prison. Some research indicates that prison administrations sometimes deliberately exacerbate racial antagonism to "divide and conquer" gangs by rewarding leaders with homosexuals of the opposite "race."

11

Land of the Walking Marriage

Lu Yuan and Sam Mitchell

Lu Yuan and Sam Mitchell co-direct the China-Yunnan Study Abroad program for the School of International Training and are honorary professors at Yunnan Normal University. Lu is a journalist and Mitchell recently received a Ph.D. in Asian history from the University of Hawaii.

> *There are so many skillful people,*
> *   but none can compare with my mother.*
> *There are so many knowledgeable people,*
> *   but none can equal my mother.*
> *There are so many people skilled at song and dance,*
> *   but none can compete with my mother.*

We first heard this folk song around a blazing fire in southwestern China in the spring of 1995. It was sung enthusiastically by women of Luoshui village—

Reprinted from *Natural History,* November 2000. Copyright © 2000 by the American Museum of Natural History.

members of the Nari, an ethnic group more commonly known to outsiders as the Mosuo. During the past few years, we have returned several times to visit these people, who celebrate women in more than song. Although the majority of China's ethnic groups follow a strong patrilineal tradition, the Mosuo emphasize matrilineal ties, with matrilineally related kin assisting one another to farm, fish, and raise children. Women also head most households and control most family property.

Marriage as other cultures know it is uncommon among the Mosuo; they prefer a visiting relationship between lovers—an arrangement they sometimes refer to in their language as *sisi* (walking back and forth). At about the age of twelve, a Mosuo girl is given a coming-of-age ceremony, and after puberty, she is free to receive male visitors. A lover may remain overnight in her room but will return in the morning to his own mother's home and his primary responsibilities. Children born from such a relationship live with their mother, and the male relatives responsible for helping to look after them are her brothers. Many children know who their fathers are, of course, but even if the relationship between father and child is quite close, it involves no social or economic obligation. And lovers can end their relationship at any time; a woman may signal her change of heart by simply no longer opening the door. When speaking Chinese, the Mosuo will call the *sisi* arrangement *zou hun* (walking marriage) or *azhu hunyin* (friend marriage, *azhu* being the Mosuo word for friend); nevertheless, the relationship is not a formal union.

Chuan-kang Shih, an anthropologist at the University of Illinois at Urbana-Champaign and an authority on the Mosuo, points out that many aspects of their family system have parallels elsewhere in the world. For example, although in most societies a husband and wife live together (usually near his relatives or hers), in others they continue to live in separate households, and one spouse must make overnight nuptial visits. Matrilineal kinship systems, in which a man looks after the interests of his sisters' children, are also well known. And although men commonly wield the power, even in matrilineal societies, women may play important political and economic roles. But the absence of a formal marital union may quite possibly be unique to the Mosuo. In this respect, only the precolonial practices of the matrilineal Nayar of southern India come close. As Shih explains, among some Nayar groups, a woman would take lovers (with due regard for social class), who would establish and maintain their relationships to her through a pattern of gift giving. Despite being expected to acknowledge paternity, the lovers incurred no obligations to their offspring. Still, the Nayar had a vestigial form of marriage: shortly before puberty, a girl would be wed to a young man; although this marriage lasted only three days and was often purely ceremonial in nature, the union marked the girl's transition to adult life and legitimized the birth of her children.

In Luoshui we stayed with thirty-year-old A Long, who runs a small guesthouse. His family consisted of his mother, grandmother, younger brother and sister, and sister's two-year-old son. Each evening A Long departed with his small overnight bag; each morning he returned to help his mother and sister.

After several days of eating with the family and becoming friendly with them, we asked A Long what he thought about the *sisi* system. "'Friend marriage' is very good," he replied. "First, we are all our mother's children, making money for her; therefore there is no conflict between the brothers and sisters. Second, the relationship is based on love, and no money or dowry is involved in it. If a couple feels contented, they stay together. If they feel unhappy, they can go their separate ways. As a result, there is little fighting." A Long told us that he used to have several lovers but started to have a stable relationship with one when she had her first child.

"Are you taking care of your children?" we asked.

"I sometimes buy candy for them. My responsibility is to help raise my sister's children. In the future, they will take care of me when I get old."

A Long's twenty-six-year-old sister, Qima, told us that the Mosuo system "is good because my friend and I help our own families during the daytime and only come together at night, and therefore there are few quarrels between us. When we are about fifty years old, we will not have 'friend marriage' anymore."

Ge Ze A Che is the leader of Luoshui, which has a population of more than 200 people, the majority of them Mosuo, with a few Han (China's majority ethnic group) and Pumi as well. He spoke proudly of this small settlement: "I have been the leader of the village for five years. There has been little theft, rape, or even argument here. 'Friend marriage' is better than the husband-wife system, because in large extended families everyone helps each other, so we are not afraid of anything. It is too hard to do so much work in the field and at home just as a couple, the way the Han do."

The Mosuo live in villages around Lugu Lake, which straddles the border between Yunnan and Sichuan provinces, and in the nearby town of Yongning. They are believed to be descendants of the ancient Qiang, an early people of the Tibetan plateau from whom many neighboring minority groups, including the Tibetans themselves, claim descent. As a result of Han expansion during the Qin dynasty (221-206 B.C.), some Qiang from an area near the Huang (Yellow) River migrated south and west into Yunnan. The two earliest mentions of the Mosuo appear during the Han dynasty (A.D. 206–222), and the Tang dynasty (618–907), in records concerning what is now southwestern China.

The Mosuo do not surface again in historical accounts until after Mongol soldiers under Kublai Khan subjugated the area in 1253. During the Yuan dynasty (1279–1368), a period of minority rule by the Mongols, the province of Yunnan was incorporated into the Chinese empire, and many Mongol soldiers settled in the Mosuo region. In fact, during the 1950s, when the government set out to classify the country's minority nationalities, several Mosuo villages surrounding Lugu Lake identified themselves as Mongol, and some continue to do so today. When we walked around the lake, as the Mosuo do each year in the seventh lunar month—a ritual believed to ensure good fortune during the coming year—we passed through villages that identified themselves variously as Mosuo, Mongol, Naxi, Pumi, and Han. The "Mongol" people we encountered dressed the same as the Mosuo and spoke the same language. Their dances and songs, too, were the same, and they sometimes even referred to themselves as Mosuo.

Tibetan Buddhism first entered the region in the late thirteenth century and has greatly influenced the lives and customs of the Mosuo. Before the area came under the control of the Communist government, at least one male from almost every family joined the monastic community. The local practice of Buddhism even incorporated aspects of the *sisi* system, although the women did the "commuting." On the eighth day of the fifth lunar month, monks traveling to Tibet for religious study would camp in front of Kaiji village. That night, each monk would be joined by his accustomed lover—a ceremonial practice believed to enable the monks to reach Lhasa safely and to succeed in completing their studies. And the local Mosuo monks, each of whom lived with his own mother's family, could also receive lovers. Such arrangements seem to defy the injunctions of many schools of Tibetan Buddhism, but by allowing the monks to live and work at home, outside the strict confines of monastic life, they helped the Mosuo maintain a stable population and ensure an adequate labor force to sustain local agriculture.

The area around Lugu Lake did not come under the full control of China's central government until 1956, seven years after the founding of the People's Republic. In 1958 and 1959, during the Great Leap Forward, the nearby monasteries, notably the one at Yongning, were badly damaged. Now, however, with a combination of government funds and donations from local people, they are slowly being rebuilt. One element of recent religious revival is the Bon tradition, which is accepted by the Dalai Lama as a school of Tibetan Buddhism but believed by many scholars to be derived from an earlier, animist tradition. During our walk around Lugu Lake, we witnessed a Bon cremation ceremony and visited the Bon temple on the eastern shore of the lake. The Mosuo also retain a shamanic and animist tradition of their own, known as Daba.

In the twentieth century, the West became acquainted with the Mosuo through the work of French ethnographers Edouard Chavannes and Jacques Bacot and through the contributions of Joseph Rock, a Vienna-born American who first journeyed to Yunnan in 1922 while on a botanical expedition. A flamboyant character, Rock traveled through remote Tibetan borderlands accompanied by trains of servants and bodyguards and equipped with such dubious necessities as a collapsible bathtub and a silver English tea set. He made the Naxi town of Lijiang his home for more than twenty years, until the victory of the Chinese Communist Party in 1949 spelled an end to foreign-funded research and missionary activity in the area.

Besides conducting botanical surveys and collecting plant and animal specimens, Rock took many photographs and became the West's foremost expert on the region's peoples and their shamanic practices. He identified the Mosuo as a subgroup of the Naxi, who, although their kinship system is patrilineal, speak a language closely related to that of the Mosuo. The Mosuo strongly contest this classification, but it has been retained by the present government, which has been reluctant to assign the Mosuo the status of a distinct minority. The Communists claim that the Mosuo do not fit the criteria for nationality status as defined for the Soviet Union by Joseph Stalin. According to Stalin, as he phrased it in a 1929 letter, "A nation is a historically constituted, stable community of people, formed on the basis of the common possession of four principal characteristics, namely: a common language, a common territory, a common economic life, and a common psychological make-up manifested in common specific features of national culture."

In keeping with Marxist interpretations of historical development, Chinese ethnologists have also regarded Mosuo society as a "living fossil," characterized by ancient marriage and family structures. This view draws on theories of social evolution formerly embraced by Western anthropologists, notably the American ethnologist Lewis Henry Morgan (1818–81). Morgan proposed that societies pass through successive natural stages of "savagery" and "barbarism" before attaining "civilization." He also proposed a sequence of marriage forms, from a hypothetical "group marriage" of brothers and sisters to monogamy. Chinese scholars have argued that a minority such as the Mosuo, with its unusual kinship system, fits into this scheme and thus validates Marxist views. Of course, the application of Morgan's theories to minority cultures in China has also enabled the Han majority to see itself as more advanced in the chain of human societal evolution. This kind of thinking, long discredited in the West, is only now beginning to be reexamined in China.

With the coming of the Cultural Revolution (1966–76), the Mosuo were pressured to change their way of life. According to Lama Luo Sang Yi Shi (a Mosuo who holds a county-government title but is primarily a spiritual leader), "during the Cultural Revolution, the governnor of Yunnan came to Yongning. He went into Mosuo homes and cursed us, saying that we were like animals, born in a mess without fathers. At that time, all of the Mosuo were forced to marry and to adopt the Han practice of monogamy; otherwise, they would be punished by being deprived of food." During this period Mosuo couples lived with the woman's family, and divorce was not permitted. But even though they held marriage certificates and lived with their wives, the men kept returning to their maternal homes each morning to work.

Luo Sang Yi criticized this attempt to change the Mosuo and explained that "at the end of the Cultural Revolution, the Mosuo soon returned to their former system of 'friend marriage.' A small family is not good for work. Also, mothers and their daughters-in-law cannot get along well."

Today the Mosuo maintain their matrilineal system and pursue *sisi* relationships. Yet how long will this remain the case? The government of Yunnan recently opened Lugu Lake to tourism, and vans full of visitors, both Chinese and foreign, are beginning to arrive. To some degree, this added exposure threatens the envelop the Mosuo in a society that is becoming increasingly homogeneous. Yet the tourists are drawn not only by the beauty of the lake but by the exotic qualities of the Mosuo people. Ironically, their unique qualities may well enable the Mosuo to endure and prosper.

We asked Ge Ze A Che, the Luoshui village leader, if tourism would change the lives of the Mosuo. "It has already changed their lives to some extent," he observed. "Our young people now like to wear Han clothes, speak Chinese, and sing Chinese songs. In the future they will lose our people's traditions and customs."

And what would happen to "friend marriage"? we wondered.

"It will also change—but very, very slowly!"

12

The Modern State: Nation-Builder or Nation-Killer?

Pierre L. van den Berghe

Pierre van den Berghe received his Ph.D. from Harvard University in 1960. He has written extensively on ethnic and race relations, sociobiology, tourism, and genocide in sub-Saharan Africa and Latin America. He is a professor of sociology and an adjunct professor of anthropology at the University of Washington.

Torrents of scholarly and political ink have flown about the modern "nation-state" (Almond and Coleman, 1960; Coleman, 1958; Coleman and Rosberg, 1964; Connor, 1990; Deutsch, 1966, 1969; Deutsch and Foltz, 1963; Emerson, 1960; Gellner, 1982; Hodgkin, 1956; Huntington, 1968; Masur, 1966; Seton-Watson,

Reprinted from *International Journal of Group Tensions* 22, no. 3 (1992), Kluwer Academic/Plenum Publishers.

1977; Smith, 1979, 1981; Snyder, 1976; Tilly, 1975; Tiryakian and Rogowski, 1985; Wallerstein, 1967; Whitaker, 1962). The strong pro-state bias of most of that literature has often been unrecognized because the authors' underlying statist premises have been implicitly shared by a broad political spectrum ranging from classical liberals to Marxists. My own approach is frankly anarchist. Simply stated, my theses are that the process euphemistically described as nation-building is, in fact, mostly nation-killing; that the vast majority of so-called "nation-states" are nothing of the sort; and that modern nationalism is a blueprint for ethnocide at best, genocide at worst.

Current Statist Myths

Let me first state, then demolish, the often unstated premises of the dominant statist tradition in the literature on nationalism:

1. States are inevitable. You need them to keep the peace.
2. Stable political regimes must rest on legitimacy. Violence is an insecure basis of statecraft.
3. Large states are better than small states because they are more economically viable. "Balkanization" and "tribalism" are bad. Nation-building is good.
4. Since states are supposed to be the political organ of the nation, it is best not to scrutinize too closely their claim to legitimacy. The distinction between state and nation is best obscured by indiscriminately referring to all states as "nation-states" (except for states one dislikes).

To which I respond:

1. States are obviously not inevitable. They have only existed for about 7,000 years of human history. We have done quite well as a species for millions of years without states. Why should we all of a sudden need them? It is true that states have been devastatingly *successful* in recent human history, because they constitute an effective way of organizing coercive violence. State-organized societies have generally won over stateless societies, and have grown rapidly through conquest. Once a state emerges in a region, it typically conquers its non-state neighbors, or forces them to develop states in self-defense. And, of course, big states gobble up small states, so that the general trend of history has been toward bigger and bigger states. The only inevitability in all this is the advantage to those who organize collective violence better. States, far from keeping the peace, wage external war on their neighbors, and parasitize their own citizens through intimidation. Let me offer, if not a definition of the state, at least an apt description of what many states do much of the time: States are killing machines run by the few to steal from the many. A state is really a big gang or mafia that extracts booty from its rivals and "protection

money" from its own citizens through the use or the threat of violence. Conversely, gangs or mafias are embryonic states.

2. Legitimacy is at best an elusive concept. It rests on a state-invented ideology to justify the existence of the state and to disguise its parasitic, exploitative and tyrannical nature. The most that can be said about legitimacy is that, to the extent that the state ideology is believed by the people, the state can economize on the use of repressive violence. It is, however, unlikely that states can fool most people most of the time, and that state domination rests primarily on legitimacy. Even many of the self-proclaimed democracies (e.g. Ancient Athens, the United States, Israel, South Africa) are or were minority governments, or *"Herrenvolk* democracies" as I called them, with political rights restricted by age, gender, legal status, religion, race or ethnicity. These states ruled not by the consent of the governed, but by the consent of the governors. George Washington's or Thomas Jefferson's slaves did not sign the Declaration of Independence or vote on the constitution. State power rests in the last analysis on violence or the threat of violence. Murder and theft are at the root of statecraft. Claims of legitimacy are merely the self-serving rationalizations of those with an interest in hiding the coercive and parasitic nature of the state.

3. If one likes states, then it stands to reason that one should also like them big and powerful. Economic viability or "economies of scale" are invoked to keep large states from breaking up. That world mafia of state-controlling elites misnamed "United Nations," for example, always rallies to the support of existing states, no matter how obnoxious, when they are threatened with "Balkanization" or "tribalism." The argument linking size of state to economic viability is sheer nonsense: What is or was economically unviable about Genoa, Bruges or Luebeck, or, today, about Lichten-stein, Singapore, Abu Dhabi, or Monaco? Yet, this inane argument has been used both to deny entities as large and prosperous as Quebec a right to independence, and to prevent basket cases like Ethiopia and Pakistan-Bangladesh from breaking up. Surely, the size of states and economic prosperity are totally independent variables. There is simply no evidence of the superiority of big states over small ones, except as killing machines. This is the only sense in which, say, Iraq is superior to Kuwait, Germany to Belgium, the Soviet Union to Poland, the United States to Grenada, South Africa to Lesoto. Large states have the ability to conquer small states, but no other evident mark of superiority.

4. The obfuscation of the distinction between state and nation, both in the social science literature and in common parlance, is not simply an innocuous piece of intellectual sloppiness. It serves the interests of ruling elites. The most common sleight of hand is that most insidious of hyphenations, the "nation-state." To be sure, there *is* such an animal: Japan, Swaziland and Somalia, for example, are genuine nation-states. The overwhelming majority of their inhabitants speak the same language, share the same culture and history, look on one another as a single ethny. In common parlance, however, "nation-state" has come to mean *any* state: Nigeria, Zaire, India, Switzerland, Yugoslavia, Canada, Trinidad, you name it. That is, the term "nation" has been made redundant to "state."

In fact, some 73 per cent of the world's independent states are multinational (by the criterion of a nation-state as an entity where 95 per cent of the population speak the same language), and, conversely, 42 per cent of ethnies or nations are split up between several states (e.g. Basques, Kurds, Koreans, Hungarians, Ewe, Bakongo and many others) (Neilsson, 1985). Until the advent of the "modern" state (using 1789 as a convenient birthdate for such an animal), it was totally unthreatening for states to recognize their multinational character. The Ottoman, Moghul, Czarist, Hapsburg, British, French, and other empires quite happily termed themselves multi-national, or *Vielvölkerstaaten* in German parlance. Even the late but unmourned Soviet Union, that gold medalist in murdering its own citizens, had the saving grace of still recognizing its multi-national character. Contemporary events clearly show how realistic that perception was.

The Nationalist State: A Fatal Mutation

The French Revolution, however, destroyed the candor of traditional empires. This brings me to the heart of my argument, namely that the modern state, inspired by the French Revolution and its ideology of nationalism and popular sovereignty, underwent a lethal mutation. In order to understand what makes modern states so ethnocidal and genocidal, let us first define what makes states modern. The modernity of states has three main ingredients, the first technological, the second ideological, and the third a corollary of the first two:

1. Modern states have an industrialized technology of destruction and mass terror.
2. Modern states legitimate their existence by claiming to represent popular sovereignty.
3. Modern states increasingly shift their lethal violence from external to internal use, and direct much of it toward ethnocide (efforts to stamp out cultural, linguistic or religious diversity) or genocide (murdering people on ethnic or racial grounds).

Let us expand on each of these points.

1. The first one is obvious. Modern state killing has become much more efficient. Not only have weapons become much better, but they can be mass-produced relatively inexpensively by a vast industrial machine (or purchased from other states or private arms dealers). States, in short, can get more and more bang for their buck, and some weapons of mass destruction are quite cheap (automatic small arms, poison gas). The French Revolution coincided roughly with the Industrial Revolution, and already Napoleon's armies could blast their foes with thousands of cannons. But the real breakthrough in mass killing came half a century later with repeating firearms, especially the machine

gun, and railways and steamship for rapid transport of troops, horses and artillery. The American Civil War, the Crimean War, and the Franco-Prussian War were among the first large-scale industrial wars, but the same technology also facilitated the last colonial expansion of Europe in Africa and Asia. The great superiority of white over black was that of the Gatlin gun over the spear.

So long as the advanced killing technology was beyond the reach of large parts of the world, as was the case until World War II, it could be used quite effectively for conquest. Now, however, small guerrilla bands with AK47's, ground-to-air missiles and plastic explosives can stalemate major powers, and upstart dictators of small countries can blackmail them with threats of unacceptable damage (as Saddam Hussein tried to do in 1990 though he overplayed his hand somewhat). Since World War I, external wars between sizeable states with comparable armaments have become a negative sum game: everybody loses. The impact of the two World Wars on all European belligerents is a case in point. Only the United States emerged as a real victor, and then mostly by getting into the war late and at a distance. Its homeland was still beyond the reach of its enemies. The latest example of the increasing unwinnability of international war is the Iran-Iraq war which was a repeat on a small scale of World War I (trench warfare, human wave attacks, poison gas) with the same outcome: stalemated exhaustion. Modern states, in short, have become vast military-industrial complexes with enormous but increasingly unusable overkill. The Soviet Union is the first major state to have collapsed in good part under the unwieldy deadweight of its military and repressive machine. The hypertrophy of the army, the police and the Gulag have produced the sclerosis of the state. The state apparatus of external and internal terror drowned in the torrent of blood it produced. The parasitic state nearly killed its host society, and ultimately committed suicide.

2. The second characteristic of modern states, noted by most analysts of nationalism (e.g. Deutsch, 1966, 1969; Emerson, 1960; Huntington, 1968; Seton-Watson, 1977; Smith, 1979; Snyder, 1976), is that, in the aftermath of the French Revolution, a new ideological fashion spread. States increasingly claimed legitimacy through "popular sovereignty," to replace the divine right of kings, paternalism, or the simple but effective notion that might is right. Now governments claimed to incarnate the "will of the people," and started creating new supposedly representative institutions. But who is "the people" whose collective will is supposedly expressed? If it has a collective will, it presumably is a community, not a mere assemblage of individuals. Social classes or estates would not do because their interests are too clearly at variance. Besides, the revolution was fought against class interests and privileges. There was, however, another preexisting collectivity, the nation, which was ideally suited to become the new legitimating myth of the state. The people was simply the nation.

Nationalism antedated, of course, the modern state but not until the 19th century did nationalism become *the* legitimating myth of the state. The new state could only be legitimate if it was the political arm of a nation, and, conversely, a nation now had a claim to statehood. If, in fact, most states had been nations or something close to it, and most nations had a state, the new ideology would have been a description of reality. However, even the birthplace and prototype of the modern state, Jacobin and Napoleonic France, did not come close to being a nation until a century or so later, as Eugene Weber (1979) has so well documented. The *grande nation* only became so by ruthlessly suppressing the languages and traditions of a dozen *petites nations* all around the periphery of Ile de France: the Flemings, Bretons, Alsacians, Corsicans, Catalans, Occitans, Basques, and others. The blueprint for nation-building was born: ethnocide (the cultural suppression of ethnic and linguistic diversity), or genocide (the physical extermination of ethnies). If the state is to become one nation, there is obviously no room for other nations.

Nation-building and nation-killing become complementary aspects of the same policy of fostering the ethnic, religious, linguistic, political and economic interests of those who control the state at the expense of all others. The state becomes identified with one ethnic group (not even necessarily a numerical majority, e.g. in South Africa the ruling Afrikaners are barely eight per cent of the population), what the Germans aptly call the *Staatsvolk*. Everyone else is subordinate.

It may be argued that domination of the state by one ethnic group is not a modern phenomenon. Was not, for instance, the Ottoman Empire a Turkish state? The answer is that, in many important ways, it was not. Non-Muslim minorities (especially Jews, Armenians and Greeks) not only had considerable autonomy and privileges under the millet system, but they were disproportionately represented in the upper echelons of government and business, as indeed were a number of foreign advisers and mercenaries. The Janissaries, the backbone of the army, were drawn from non-Muslim, non-Turkic groups. Christians and Jews had full freedom of worship. Everyone was free to speak his own language, and Greek, for instance, continued to be widely spoken in urban areas. Istanbul was a Babel of peoples and tongues. The ruling class of the Empire, in short, was largely indifferent as to what languages people spoke so long as they remained docile and paid their taxes.

The fatal mutation came during World War I when the Ottoman Empire disintegrated into would-be national states, half-a-dozen Arab ones under British and French tutelage (including Palestine and Lebanon, future hotbeds of endless nationalist conflicts). The rump of the Empire became the Turkish Republic under the militant nationalists known as the Young Turks. The outcome was the first great genocide of the 20th century, the murder of over a million Armenians (Hovannisian, 1986). Since then, the history of Turkey has been one of intolerance towards all non-Turkish minorities, even Muslim ones like the Kurds, whose very existence is denied. There are no Kurds, the Turkish government tells the rest of the world, only "mountain Turks." As for the Armenian genocide, it never happened if one is to believe the Turkish government; lots of people died during the war, including some Armenians, but that was just the unfortunate consequence of the inevitable turmoil of war according to official Turkish historiography. Turks too suffered. (One is reminded of

Himmler's commiseration for his SS who had such a tough job running concentration camps.)

Traditional empires were generally tolerant of, or at least indifferent to, ethnic, linguistic or even religious diversity. For the most part, they even rejoiced in their subjects' diversity. Colonial India, Nigeria, or Congo were made-to-order for a policy of dividing and ruling. The more tribes, castes and religions, the merrier, as far as the ruling class was concerned. Even the French were much less than half-hearted in their supposed policy of assimilation in Asia or Africa. The French state was ruthlessly assimilationist within the *hexagone* (metropolitan France). In Senegal, Madagascar, Indochina or even Algeria, it never really believed that all those dark colonials were potential Frenchmen. Systematic suppression of ethnic diversity is the hallmark of modern nationalism. Colonial empires can live quite happily with a Babel of tongues and cultures.

3. As a corollary of the first and second characteristics of modern states, there has been a shift from external to internal violence. As weaponry became more and more destructive and equally distributed between states so that even third-rate powers could threaten massive destruction, external wars became less and less attractive and winnable. The Vietnams and Afghanistans of the world can reduce superpowers to bloody and costly stalemates and even defeats. Even the "victory" of the Gulf War is a Pyrrhic one: Kuwait was destroyed before it was saved. At the same time, the would-be nation-states are riddled with hostile, captive nations within their own borders which they seek to subdue in the name of nation-building.

The figures are eloquent. Harff and Gurr (1987) who compiled a necrology of mass state violence since 1945, document that, at a minimum, two thirds of all people killed by states have been internal victims of genocides or what they call "politicides." Estimates of internal bloodbaths yield totals of 6.8 to 16.3 million victims (megadeaths, for short) between 1945 and 1987, depending on whose figures one accepts. This compared to 3.34 megadeaths in international wars between 1945 and 1980. There were six internal megadeath events by their account, involving the USSR, the People's Republic of China, Indonesia, Pakistan-Bangladesh, Kampuchia, and Afghanistan. The one clearly international event in the same league was the Iran-Iraq War, not included in the Harff and Gurr statistics since these stop at 1980 for international conflicts. Harff and Gurr have a third category for "colonial and civil wars" which included such protracted conflicts as the Indochina War and the Nigerian Civil War, which made another 3.13 megadeaths. Many of these civil wars were scarcely distinguishable in nature from politicides and genocides, or at least included within them major massacres by governments of unarmed civilians within their own state boundaries.

Whichever way one classifies acts of state-sponsored murder, it is clear that, since World War II, something like three quarters of all fatalities were caused by states butchering their own citizens in genocides or politicides. Ten megadeaths for the period seems a reasonable middle estimate.

The "Nation-State" A Legitimation Myth

My analysis will no doubt displease and offend many. First, state-controlling elites insist that their ethnocides and genocides are internal affairs, and that world order rests on governments giving each other *carte blanche* in butchering their own citizens. Such was obviously the dominant "gentlemen's agreement" at the United Nations (a sad misnomer for Squabbling States). In that sanctimonious forum of state-controlling elites, delegates have achieved near-unanimity on only one issue: to make sure that the Genocide Convention would remain, quite literally, a dead letter (Kuper, 1981, 1982, 1985). Second, most social scientists have done their best to befuddle the issue of nationalism for the benefit of state-controlling elites. It is to that scholarly conspiracy of befuddlement that I shall now turn. Political and other social scientists could easily have called the bluff of state-controlling elites calling themselves "nation-states," yet scholars seldom did because of their own statist bias.

How did social scientists cope with the embarrassing fact that most of the world's states are not nations, nor most nations, states (Neilsson, 1985)? The simplest ploy was the uncritical acceptance of the hyphenation "nation-state." The unexamined confusion characterizes at least 90 per cent of post World War II authors on nationalism and the state. But there were more ingenious forms of befuddlement as well. One is the subjectivist, or "instrumentalist" view of ethnicity and nationalism, which denies the ethny or nation any external or objective reality, and holds that ethnicity or nationhood is whatever people, especially political elites, say it is. If Mobutu says Zaire is a nation, then by definition it is. This radical subjectivist view of nations as the figment of political imaginations in the service of political gains is, in fact, the dominant position in social science.

Another ploy was to redefine nationalism, or to distinguish different types of nationalism in different parts of the world or in different periods. The Africanist literature, especially in the 1960's, is a good example of these mental convolutions (Coleman and Rosberg, 1964; Hodgkin, 1956; Wallerstein, 1967; Young, 1965). Many analysts observed that "nationalism" in Africa was something different from what it was in Europe, yet they overwhelmingly accepted the misnomer. It is plainly grotesque to characterize as "nationalist" the civilian or military kleptocrats who have appropriated African states for private gain, and typically live on incomes 100 times their countries' average, and equally preposterous to call these countries "nation-states" when nine tenths of them are patchworks of ethnies thrown together by artificial colonial boundaries. What we have in nearly all of Africa are small Western-educated elites who inherited an alien, colonial system of government; perpetuated their minority rule through graft, corruption and violence; and appropriated all organs of state control for private exploitation and gain, through a complex network of nepotism and ethnic favoritism. This is about as "nationalist" as the Sicilian mafia, the Medellin drug cartel or the Moghul Empire.

Why then, did scholars persistently misuse these labels? The answer is suggested by the prevalent use of another set of terms dear to Africanists: tribe and tribalism. These terms, be it noted, are seldom used in political analysis, except in Africa and in aboriginal North America. In Africa, they have clearly derogatory connotations. Nationalism is good, modern and progressive; tribalism is bad, traditional and reactionary. African politicians are praised for seeking to maintain "national unity" against the divisive threat of the primitive, atavistic savagery of tribal hatreds. All this invidious vocabulary used to describe African politics and all the supposedly unique features of African conflicts are revealed as an ideological smokescreen when one realizes that what is called "tribalism" in Africa is in fact authentic nationalism, while the so-called "nationism" of African states and their ruling elites is nothing of the sort.

Such perverse misuse of terms was sustained by a multi-national coalition of elites. Africanist scholars (mostly from Europe or North America) have been conditioned to look at Africa through a racist prism that made it seem eminently sensible to label groups "tribes" if their members were darkly pigmented, and "nations" if light in color. Thus, the Amhara, Yoruba or Zulu are tribes; the Finns, Danes or Croats are nations. African elites, on the other hand, were also happy with that terminology because it justified their murderous repression of dissident movements as progressive, and appeared to legitimate their claim to be ruling "nation-states." Colonial prejudices and neocolonial interests converged on the perpetuation of analytical obfuscation. The misuse of terms made it easy, for instance, to apply a double standard of judgment to the use of repressive violence in South Africa and the rest of the continent.

A state like South Africa, which never pretended to be a nation, can be safely condemned as reactionary for maintaining an archaic colonial system of racial segregation and ethnic domination, even though its level of murderous repression is moderate compared to the state-sponsored genocidal orgies perpetuated during recent decades in Burundi, Ethiopia, the Sudan, Liberia, Cambodia, Iran, Iraq, or Syria. Sure, the South African police operates death squads and murders political prisoners in detention (or, at least, did until recently), but it does not blanket Bantustans in mustard gas as, for instance, Saddam Hussein did with Kurds in 1988. Sure the South African government periodically bulldozes black urban settlements, but it never forced marched, executed and starved hundreds of thousands of people out of Soweto as the Khmer Rouge did in Phnom-Penh. South Africa has only known one major episode of state-encouraged genocide: the extermination campaigns against the San ("Bushmen") in the Cape from the late 17th through the mid-19th centuries. South Africa is a Herrenvolk democracy, an unwieldy hybrid of a parliamentary regime for the *Staatsvolk*, the Afrikaners, and a garden-variety settler-colonial regime for the black population. It would be a more murderous state if it claimed to be a nation-state.

The Routinization of Genocide

Notwithstanding, then, the scholarly tradition that would make the Nazi Holocaust a unique or at least exceptional event, the genocide against Jews in the Second World War was merely one of the largest and best documented genocides unleashed by modern nationalism. It was, in fact, only one of *two* genocides perpetuated by the Nazi regime, the other being that of the Rom ("Gypsies"), and one of hundreds of genocidal massacres by scores of states during the last two centuries. If one defines genocide as a deliberate state-sponsored or supported attempt to decimate large numbers of people on the basis of race or ethnicity, by direct execution, death camps, death marches, induced famines or other methods designed to kill, then the instances certainly run into the hundreds.

The majority of them are small-scale, but nonetheless highly successful events, involving the virtual extermination of small marginal groups that only a few anthropologists have ever heard of, and who therefore can be killed silently and away from the spotlight of unwanted publicity. This has been the fate of countless "aboriginal" groups in Australia, Southern Africa and America, and continues to this date in Amazonia. But even massive genocides involving hundreds of thousands or even millions of "civilized" victims in Europe have been recently "rediscovered," e.g., the deliberate decimation by starvation, exposure and unchecked epidemics of perhaps up to 800,000 German prisoners of war in U.S. and French camps in 1945, an atrocity almost certainly attributable to Dwight Eisenhower (Bacque, 1989) and the genocide by famine of between three and eight million Ukrainians by Stalin in 1932–33 (Conquest, 1986; Commission on the Ukraine Famine, 1988). Hitler, Stalin and Eisenhower all belong in the great fraternity of leaders of genocidal states. The terror and horror of mass genocidal killing are not aberrations of the modern state; they are in the very nature of it. We live in an era of routinized holocausts. If *the* Holocaust has a distinctive characteristic it is that it was conducted with Teutonic *Gründlichkeit;* otherwise, it was fairly routine.

Some Hints on Genocide Prevention

Is genocide inevitable in modern states? Obviously not; not all states are genocidal all the time. There are alternatives, and it is important not only to spell them out, but to understand their limits.

1. Small, weak states with citizen-armies or no armies at all tend to be less lethal than large, strong ones with mercenary armies. This is especially true of small states in the fear-shadow of big ones, like Luxembourg or Switzerland. However, small weak states that are effectively isolated from pressures by neighboring states, and even from news coverage, can conduct genocide with impunity, as shows, for instance, by Burundi.

It is also true that states can be so weak as to be unable to prevent orgies of communal violence that are largely privately sponsored. Sri Lanka is a good example, but, even though most of the ethnic massacres were not state-sponsored, the state provoked Tamil nationalism by adopting ethnic quota policies systematically favoring the Sinhalese. Lebanon is another case in point, though one greatly complicated by Syrian, Palestinian and Israeli intervention.

2. True nation-states are, by definition, less likely to be internally genocidal, because of lack of targets. Thus, given an acceptance of nationalism as the basis of legitimation for states, the break-up of multinational empires into smaller, weaker, mono-ethnic states is desirable. Not only the rest of the world, but many groups within the former Soviet Union, for example, are breathing more peacefully since the empire began to break down. However, even genuine nation-states can find small minorities to scapegoat. Jews and Rom (Gypsies) together made up under one per cent of Nazi Germany's 1938 population, and, furthermore, most German Jews were so assimilated that, objectively, they were in no sense an alien nation. Still, the Final Solution was only implemented after German conquest incorporated millions of foreign Jews. The Holocaust was overwhelmingly an external, not an internal genocide. Of the two greatest state killers of this century, Nazi Germany and the Stalinist Soviet Union, the former, a nation-state, was externally genocidal, while the latter, a multi-national empire, was internally so (to the tune of 30 to 60 million, according to the most credible estimates). The seeming German exception, in fact, confirms our second proposition.

3. Short of a break-up into independent nation-states, multi-national states best approximate a Swiss model of a loose confederation of autonomous ethnic or even sub-ethnic groups, like the Swiss canton. Confederal solutions of local autonomy are especially attractive where ethnic groups are largely territorialized as in the case in countries like Belgium, Switzerland, Yugoslavia, the Soviet Union, Canada (between Angloand Franco-Canadians), India, and many others. The more territorially dispersed ethnic groups are, and the more multi-ethnic areas (especially *urban* areas) become, the thornier ethnic problems grow. The lesson is that states should not devolve power to local authorities, but discourage colonization settlements, e.g. of Russians in non-Russian parts of the Soviet Union, of Jews in the West Bank of Palestine, or of Javanese in Borneo and West Irian, to mention only three state-sponsored designs to extend the domination of the Staatsvolk to ethnically alien areas. Every colonization scheme contains the seeds of ethnic conflict and potential genocide.

4. What to do about the world's many ethnically scrambled areas where neat territorial partition along natural lines is not possible or would be too costly? Even then, partition may turn out not to be such a bad solution, as the relatively successful Cypriot example shows (imposed though it was by Turkish arms). Over a third of the island's Greek and Turkish population had to move at great personal cost and suffering, but ethnic violence has ceased since partition and the creation of two ethnic micro-states. Palestinian partition might also have worked, had it not been undone by Israeli conquest in the 1967 war. However, let us admit that partition is often unrealistic and undesirable.

There are many types of ethnically and/or racially "scrambled" situations, each with its special kinds of problems: post-slavery situations such as in the Caribbean, Brazil and the United States; massive waves of immigration as in Canada, Argentina, Australia and the United States; temporary labor migration as in many African and European cities, "middleman" mercantile communities as the overseas Chinese and Indians in South East Asia, Eastern Africa and the Caribbean, and so on. The very diversity of such situations defies simple solutions, and state policies have varied enormously, with equally diverse consequences. At one extreme have been genocidal massacres (e.g. of Chinese in Indonesia); encouraged terrorism to foster mass flight (e.g. of Palestinians in Israel during wars); and state-managed expulsions (e.g. of Asians from Uganda under Idi Amin). At the other end of the spectrum, some states have institutionalized what Lijphart (1977) has called "consociationism." In countries like Belgium, Canada, Yugoslavia, and others, the state has an official policy not only of federalism based on multi-lingualism and recognition of ethnic distinctions, but also a system of ethnic proportional representation in the organs of government.

In between these extremes of intolerance and encouragement of ethnic diversity fall a wide range of state policies. Some states, notably France and most of Latin America (with the partial exception of Paraguay), have resolutely ignored cultural and linguistic diversity and pushed through the dominant language and culture through official monolingualism and propagation of the "national" culture of the ruling elite. State-encouraged assimilation to the dominant ethny is the essence of the much vaunted "nation-building" efforts of many governments and can itself range from passive ethnocide through "benign neglect" of minority cultures presumed to be on a "natural" road to extinction, all the way to the active genocide of prohibiting the use of languages, forcing people to change their names, banning cultural practices, and imposing ethnically-based legal restrictions on property-holding, marriage, trading, employment and so on.

It is also frequently the case that the same country can simultaneously or sequentially practice several forms of repression ranging from genocide to "benign neglect." E.g. the United States has sequentially used the whole panoply of repression against American Indians: genocide, expulsions, land "relocations," land theft, linguistic and cultural suppression, kidnaping of children in government schools, encapsulation into internal colonies ("reservations"), the "benign neglect" of the "termination policy," and the parody of "national autonomy" based on continuously broken "treaty rights."

In a slightly different mode, some countries have practiced different forms and degrees of repression against different ethnic groups. For instance, Turkey has conducted genocide against Armenians, and repeated attempts at forceful ethnocide against Kurds, but has been relatively tolerant of Jews. The variations, in short, are legion (Horowitz, 1985; van den Berghe, 1981, 1990; Wirsing, 1981). Even supposedly benign policies such as "reverse discrimination" or "affirmative action" have frequently had adverse consequences for their supposed beneficiaries, and have turned out to be, in fact, policies of tokenism and internal colonialism (Glazer, 1975; van den Berghe, 1981).

Toward a Denationalized State

Assuming that one seeks tolerance of ethnic diversity and the maximum preservation of individual rights to conduct one's life through the linguistic and cultural medium of one's choice, a few prescriptions and caveats emerge from past experiences of many states. Ideally, the state should not be associated with any particular group, but should be the neutral, common property of all of its citizens. I am simply advocating an extension of the principle of secularization in the religious sphere to language and other cultural domains. Much as the state should tolerate all religions but be associated with none, the state should also be "denationalized."

This is a difficult prescription, especially in the linguistic sphere, because, while it is easy enough to transact government business without reference to religion, one must use some language to communicate. Almost inevitably, the language of the majority (or of the ruling elite) becomes dominant. The state, however, has no need to declare any language "national," and no mandate to push, protect or even encourage any language at the expense of others. Competing languages operate in a sort of marketplace of utility in which the state best not interfere, except perhaps in the field of education, where schooling at all levels should be made available in the languages of choice of individuals (or their parents), and in government services, which should also be available insofar as possible in the language of choice of those served.

This prescription implies a flexible, demand-based policy of pragmatic multi-lingualism in ethnically mixed areas, wherein the state would refrain from either declaring any languages official or allocating any definite language rights to officially recognized ethnic groups, but simply provide multi-lingual facilities to people *as individuals.* For instance, in the Sun Belt of the United States with large Hispanic minorities, any parent, whether Hispanic or Anglo, would have the practical option of sending his or her children to a Spanish-medium, English-medium, or bilingual school, of taking standardized tests in either language, and so on. This is quite distinct from conceding a special right to Hispanics to go to Spanish-medium schools, for such a policy of special rights to minority groups is inevitably resented, and frequently carries a stigma of inferiority for the minority group.

The state then should not only denationalize. It should also incorporate all of its citizens strictly as *individuals,* endowed with strictly equal rights, without any official recognition granted to any group affiliation. Ethnic or racial self-identification should be protected by the state as an individual option (provided it does not entail discrimination against others), but the state itself should pay no attention to the way people choose to identify themselves, much less base policies on such identifications. In fact, the state should not even ask ethnic or racial questions on its census, any more than it should ask religious questions. Ethnicity, in short, should be entirely in the private sphere, as is religion in secular states.

A corollary of the above is that states should also refrain from ethnically or racially based policies of granting special rights or preferences to groups it sees as in need of redress or remedial action. Reverse discrimination, quota systems, and "affirmative action" based on race or ethnicity, whatever their purported benevolence, almost inevitably backfire because they are widely resented by supposedly privileged groups, demean minority groups, result in tokenism, detract from broader class-based solutions to systemic inequalities, set minority groups against each other, benefit the already privileged within the disadvantaged groups, and generally exacerbate ethnic and racial conflicts and perpetuate prejudices. Redressive policies should be based on *class*, not race or ethnicity, and should follow social democratic principles, such as progressive taxation, need-based welfare programs, and the like, with qualifications strictly by individual socioeconomic criteria, not group affiliation.

The French and American Revolutions created the secular state, and that was probably their greatest advance over the preceding age of religious tyranny and conflict. When the state stopped taking sides and interfering in religious conflicts, the latter largely withered into the sphere of private competition. The same revolutions unfortunately created the monster of the nationalist state. Two hundred years of state-sponsored ethnocide and genocide are quite enough. If we must have states, which I am not prepared to concede, let them be small, weak, and hemmed in by broad supra-state economic agencies like the European Community. Above all, let them be not only secular but denationalized. Genuine nation-states are bad enough in their parochialism. Multi-national states that masquerade as nations have such a lethal historical record that they can no longer be tolerated. At the very least, they should be exposed with favor toward none.

Acknowledgment

This article is a revision of a paper presented at the First International Congress on Prejudice, Discrimination and Conflict, held in Jerusalem on July 1–4, 1991.

References

Almond, G. A., & Coleman, J. S., eds. (1960). *The Politics of the Developing Areas.* Princeton: Princeton University Press.

Bacque, J. (1989). *Other Losses.* Don Mills, Ont.: Stoddart.

Coleman, J. S. (1958). *Nigeria, Background to Nationalism.* Berkeley: University of California Press.

Coleman, J. S., & Rosberg, C., eds. (1964). *Political Parties and National Integration in Tropical Africa.* Berkeley: University of California Press.

Commission on the Ukraine Famine (1988). *Investigation of the Ukraine Famine, 1932–1933, Report to Congress.* Washington: United States Government Printing Office.

Connor, W. (1990). When Is a Nation? *Ethnic and Racial Studies 13,* 92–103.

Conquest, R. (1986). *The Harvest of Sorrow.* New York: Oxford University Press.

Deutsch, K. W. (1966). *Nationalism and Social Communication.* New York: MIT Press.

——— (1969). *Nationalsim and Its Alternatives.* New York: Knopf.

Deutsch, K. W., & Foltz, W. J., eds. (1963) *National Building.* New York: Atherton.

Emerson, R. (1960). *From Empire to Nation.* Cambridge, Mass.: Harvard University Press.

Gellner, E. (1982). *Nations and Nationalism.* Oxford: Basil Blackwell.

Glazer, N. (1975). *Affirmative Discrimination.* New York: Basic Books.

Harff, B., & Gurr, T. R. (1987). Genocides and Politicides Since 1945, *Internet on the Holocaust and Genocide,* December, Special Issue 13:1–5.

Hodgkin, T. (1956). *Nationalism in Colonial Africa.* London: Muller.

Horowitz, D. L. (1985). *Ethnic Groups in Conflict.* Berkeley: University of California Press.

Hovannisian, R., ed. (1986). *The Armenian Genocide in Perspective.* New Brunswick: Transaction Books.

Huntington, S. P. (1968). *Political Order in Changing Societies.* New Haven: Yale University Press.

Kuper, L. (1981). *Genocide.* New York: Penguin Books.

——— (1982). *International Action Against Genocide.* London: Minority Rights Group.

——— (1985). *The Prevention of Genocide.* New Haven: Yale University Press.

Lijphart, A. (1977). *Democracy in Plural Societies.* New Haven: Yale University Press.

Masur, G. (1966). *Nationalism in Latin America.* New York: Macmillan.

Nielsson, G. P. (1985). States and "Nation-Groups," A Global Taxonomy, in E. A. Tiryakian & R. Rogowski, eds., *New Nationalisms of the Developed West.* Boston: Allen and Unwin.

Seton-Watson, H. (1977). *Nations and States.* London: Methuen.

Smith, A. D. (1979). *Nationalism in the Twentieth Century.* Oxford: Martin Robertson.

——— (1981). *The Ethnic Revival.* Cambridge: Cambridge University Press.

Snyder, L. (1976). *The Varieties of Nationalism, A Comparative View.* Hinsdale, Ill.: Dryden Press.

Tilly, C., ed. (1976). *The Formation of National States in Western Europe.* Princeton: Princeton University Press.

Tiryakian, E. A., & Rogowski, R., eds. (1985). *New Nationalisms of the Developed West.* Boston: Allen and Unwin.

van den Berghe, P. L. (1981). *The Ethnic Phenomenon.* New York: Elsevier.

van den Berghe, P. L., ed. (1990). *State Violence and Ethnicity.* Niwot: University Press of Colorado.

Wallerstein, I. (1967). *Africa, The Politics of Unity.* New York: Random House.

Weber, E. (1979). *Peasants into Frenchmen, The Modernization of Rural France: 1870–1914.* London: Chatto and Windus.

Whitaker, A. P. (1962). *Nationalism in Latin America, Past and Present.* Gainesville: University of Florida Press.

Wirsing, R., ed. (1981). *Protection of Ethnic Minorities.* New York: Pergamon Press.

Young, C. (1965). *Politics in the Congo, Decolonization and Independence.* Princeton: Princeton University Press.

13

Language and Social Identity

Rodolfo Stavenhagen

Rodolfo Stavenhagen, who has an international reputation as a development anthropologist, is on the faculty of El Colegio de México. He is also the coordinator of the United Nations university project on ethnic minorities and human and social development.

Languages shape culture and society in many important ways. They are, for example, the vehicles for literary and poetic expressions, the instruments whereby oral history, myths and beliefs are shared by a community, and transmitted from generation to generation. Just as an Indian without land is a dead Indian (as the World Council of Indigenous Peoples states), so also an ethnic community without a language is a dying community. This was well understood by the romantic nationalists of the 19th and 20th centuries who strove for a revival of "national" languages as part of the politics of nationalism.

Reprinted from United Nations *Work in Progress* 13, no. 2 (December 1990).

On the other hand, language has always been an instrument of conquest and empire. Nebrija, a 15th-century Castillian grammarian and adviser to Queen Isabella I of Spain, published his Spanish grammar the same year Columbus reached America, and he advised his queen to use the language as an instrument for the good government of the empire. Both the Spanish Crown and the Church took the advice to heart—and Spanish became one of the universal languages of the modern world. So did English, of course, for the British Empire knew well the power of the word as an instrument of world power.

In the process of colonization, the languages of the colonized peoples—especially if unwritten—were usually downgraded to mere "dialects," a term which connotes something less than a full-fledged structured language, and therefore casts doubt on the status of the culture which uses it. Thus indigenous and tribal peoples are still widely considered today to speak only dialects and not languages—a position frequently shared by government bureaucrats.

This is, of course, linguistic nonsense, but it carries a political message. As some anonymous with has expressed it: a language is a dialect with an army. Or, to put it in another way, a dominant group is able to impose its language on subordinate groups. Linguistic dominance is more often than not an expression of political and economic domination. To be sure, there are exceptions: in Africa, Asia and the Caribbean, there are a number of *linguae francae*, vehicular languages used for trade and commerce which do not necessarily denote political domination.

In the predominant statist view, stressing national unity, assimilation and development, the languages of indigenous and tribal peoples have usually been destined to disappear. Government policies have generally been designed to help this process along. In most countries, indigenous languages are not given legal recognition, are not used in official administrative and judicial dealings, and are not taught in schools. The people who do use them are discriminated against and treated by the nonindigenous as outsiders, foreigners, barbarians, primitives, and so on.

Very often, the men of a tribe or indigenous community, who move around in the outside world for economic reasons, learn the official or national language of a country and become bilingual. Women tend to be more monolingual, which increases their isolation and the discrimination which they suffer. Small children, before school age, speak the maternal language—but often, as soon as they start school, are not allowed to speak it in class. Observers have noted that this can create serious psychological and learning problems among the school-age children of many indigenous and tribal peoples. Indeed because of language and other forms of discrimination, families sometimes avoid sending their children to official or missionary schools at all.

A United Nations examination of language practices noted that the policies followed by a great many governments were based on earlier assumptions that "indigenous populations, cultures and languages would disappear naturally or by absorption into other segments of the population and the national culture." Now, however, judging by their effects, such policies are beginning to be recognized as not well grounded; public schooling directed toward the achievement of these policies has been severely questioned.

As a result of policies of persecution and general attitudes of discrimination against them, many indigenous peoples have internalized the negative attitudes of the dominant society against their languages and cultures. Particularly when they leave their communities, they tend to deny their identity and feel ashamed of being "aboriginal," or "native" or "primitive."

But hiding an identity is not always possible, given that many ethnic and cultural differences are accompanied by biological distinctions. This has been particularly the case in European settler societies where the biological differences between the upper classes and the indigenous populations are particularly visible. It is less so in societies which have undergone a process of racial intermarriage and mixing, as in many Asian and Latin American countries.

In recent years, indigenous and tribal peoples have begun to resist the forced disappearance of their languages and cultures. And there has been a slow but growing awareness among social scientists, humanists, educators and even politicians that the maintenance of indigenous languages within the concept of cultural pluralism is not necessarily undesirable for a given country.

One of the questions being debated currently among linguistic specialists is whether language rights should be considered human rights. Article 27 of the International Covenant on Civil and Political Rights establishes that persons belonging to ethnic, religious or linguistic minorities shall not be denied the right to use their own language. However, organizations of indigenous peoples around the world refuse to be categorized among "ethnic minorities." This is one of the reasons why a specific declaration of indigenous rights is being prepared in the specialized UN bodies.

Language rights certainly seem to be a major issue among indigenous organizations. At the regional level, for example, periodic inter-American indigenist congresses (which are affiliated with the Organization of American States) have reaffirmed for several years the linguistic rights of the indigenous populations in the Western Hemisphere. UNESCO has also underlined the importance of the use of vernacular languages as an integral part of the cultural policies of states, particularly as regards education for minority groups. A number of countries have recently changed their traditional postures of discrimination against, and the neglect of, indigenous and tribal minority languages, and have designed policies to protect and promote these languages.

In a number of countries, indigenous organizations—and sometimes sympathetic governments—are experimenting with new linguistic and educational policies which take indigenous claims into account. In order to teach the vernacular language, however, many unwritten indigenous languages have had to be turned into written tongues. Alphabets have had to be prepared; educational materials in the vernacular have had to be provided, and teachers have had to be trained.

But this can be a lengthy and complicated process, and among educators and government officials the debates continue as to the relative merits of one or another kind of educational system—monolingual or multilingual. In countries where there exist myriad small indigenous linguistic groups, governments argue that such educational innovations are costly and basically inefficient. In addition, it is often feared that fragmenting the educational systems along linguistic lines is a potential threat to national unity. In these countries, if a majority national language exists, government policy tends to favour teaching only the national or official language.

In other countries, where the indigenous communities are large—and particularly if they have a certain amount of political clout—the education in indigenous languages is more likely to become accepted. In most countries where indigenous language schooling is taking root, bilingual education tends to be the norm. The indigenous language is taught together with the official or national language.

Just what the pedagogical mix between the various languages is depends on local conditions. Some authors consider formal schooling in an indigenous language as merely a step towards the appropriation of the official or national language. Others consider it as an end in itself—which is what the indigenous peoples themselves claim. In most countries, the teaching of an indigenous language is carried out only at the lower levels of elementary schooling. In others it also covers up through secondary levels and higher technical schools.

A linked, but much more complicated, educational problem is making bilingual schooling truly bicultural or intercultural. School children in urban industrial environments formally learn about their own larger "national" culture. Children in indigenous schools must take the reverse path: learning about their own particular cultures and identities, along with what they are taught about their "total society." This poses a formidable task for educational planners as to curriculum development, preparation of textbooks, reading and audio-visual materials, and so forth.

Indigenous peoples have been claiming the right to establish and control their own educational institutions, which means exercising control over their own curriculum, and educational contents. In some countries this is being achieved, and, in many areas, interesting educational experiments are taking place. In other countries—and particularly in the poorer third world countries—this must be the government's responsibility. But, as I have noted, governments are not always eager to undertake such innovation, particularly because they have been identified so long with assimilationist approaches.

The individual human rights spelled out in the Universal Declaration of Human Rights are now, forty years after their proclamation, generally accepted as international *customary* law. Obviously, indigenous peoples enjoy these same rights. There is a growing consensus, however, that the various international human rights instruments are not enough to guarantee the survival and protection of indigenous peoples around the world—particularly in the face of accelerated economic, social and cultural change. Thus the need for the definition of *collective* economic, social and cultural human rights is now becoming increasingly recognized.

14

Forms of Address: How Their Social Functions May Vary

Salikoko S. Mufwene

Salikoko S. Mufwene, a native of the Democratic Republic of the Congo, came to the United States in 1974 as a graduate student at the University of Chicago. He received his Ph.D. in linguistics in 1979 and is now a professor of linguistics at his old alma mater. Previously he taught at the University of the West Indies in Jamaica and at the University of Georgia. Among his research interests is the relationship between language and culture, as well as pidgin and Creole speech.

The point of view presented in this essay is primarily Bantu, one of the several groups of sub-Saharan Africans typically characterized as black. Moreover, the

Reprinted from *Distant Mirrors: America as a Foreign Culture,* edited by Philip R. De Vita and James D. Armstrong (2001), Wadsworth.

outlook is that of a person who grew up in the central African colony of Belgian Congo during its transition to the independent nation of Zaire (called the Democratic Republic of the Congo since 1997) and was educated in a system that fosters an interesting coexistence of colonial European and local African cultures. From a sociolinguistic point of view, French, inherited from the colonial days as the official language and the medium of education from the fourth grade up to higher education, has been adapted to convey this marriage of African, and colonial European cultures heavily anchored in the African tradition.

In this essay, I show how this background affected my reaction over fifteen years ago to English forms of address, as used at a major midwestern American university. With time, I have also learned that the customs described in this essay do not apply universally to the overall American society. However, I think that these first impressions reflect best my then unacculturated perception of a facet of American culture.

The term "form of address" is used in this essay as much for names, like *Peter, Mary,* and *Bob,* as for titles, like *Mr., Mrs., Dr.,* and *Professor,* which are normally used before last or full names, for example, *Mr. (Paul) Simon* or *Dr. (Alice) Rosenfeld.* The term is also used for other titles such as *sir* and *ma'am,* normally used without a name; for kinship terms such as *Dad, Mom,* and *son* used to address relatives; for pet names such as *buttercup* and *cupcake;* or for any word used to address a person. Ethnographically, these forms of address specify the relation between the speaker and the addressee (for example, pals, professionals, parent-child, lovers) and the terms of their interaction (for example, distant, close, intimate), depending sometimes on the specific circumstances of the communication. To take an American example, a person named *Alice Rosenfeld* may be addressed in various ways, depending on context. She may be addressed as *Dr. Rosenfeld* in formal professional interaction, as *Mrs.* or *Ms. Rosenfeld* in situations where she is not well known, as *Mom* by her children, as *Alice* by her husband and colleagues in places where professional relations are not formal, and as *dear, darling,* or *honey* by her husband in intimate interaction.

I will restrict my observations on the American system to the usage of forms of address after the first time people have been introduced to each other. I will ignore those situations where preestablished relationships might allow usage of pet names and kinship titles, for instance, the title *uncle* extended to friends of the speaker's parents or blood uncles. However, it will help to provide more general background information about myself at this point, so that the reader may understand my original shock at how Americans address each other, at least at the university I attended.

In my Bantu background, addressees' names are often avoided in quite a variety of situations in order to express deference and/or intimacy. For instance, in the Bantu vernacular languages, people of the same age as one's parents are addressed by the same titles as the parents of the same sex, with the terms *papa* or *tata* (father) or *mama* (mother) prefixed to their names to express deference, for example, *Papa Kaniki* or *Mama Moseka*. These honorifics (that is, special forms of address for respect) are also used alone, without a name, to express both deference and intimacy when the speaker knows the addressee closely. For instance, in Kikongo-Kituba (my regional lingua franca), a close relation of the speaker's family who is of approximately the same age as, or older than, his or her father may be addressed as follows: *Papa, ebwe?* (Papa, how are you?)

When used alone to address strangers, the honorifics *papa* and *mama* are simple markers of politeness corresponding to the English honorifics *sir* and *ma'am*, used without a name, or to the honorifics *Mr., Mrs., Ms., Dr.,* and the like prefixed to the last names in formal interaction. These honorifics also are often used for addressees of the age group of the speaker's children as affective forms of address, corresponding to, for instance, the use of *son* by a nonkin. Thus, the sentence *Papa, ebwe?* used by an adult to a child is affective and may be translated idiomatically as "How are you, son/darling/dear?" All these Bantu forms of address fit in a system in which addressees' names are generally avoided, a practice to which I return below.

People of the age group of the speaker's older siblings are addressed in Kikongo-Kituba either by prefixing the kinship honorific *yaya* (older sibling) to their names for deference or by using the title alone for both deference and intimacy, for example, *Yaya Kalala*. Ethnographically, this corresponds in American English to addressing such a close relation by his or her first name or nickname.

A number of older male persons are assimilated to uncles and are addressed on the same pattern as above with the kinship honorific *noko* (uncle), for example, *Noko Mukoko*. However, note that many of the people addressed with this honorific would not be addressed with the honorific *uncle* in American English, since they may not be close friends of the speaker's parents or blood uncles.

Adult close friends often address one another by their professional titles, if these are considered as achievements (for example, *Munganga, ebwe?* [Dr. (MD), how are you?]), or by their nicknames or play names (for example, *Mbongo mpasi, ebwe?* [Hard Money, how are you?]). This custom is to express intimacy. In the case of professional titles, close associates bear the responsibility of setting up examples for others to follow; deference starts at home. Once more, usage of addressees' names is generally restricted to situations where it is absolutely necessary to make clear which person is being addressed, for instance, when more than one person in the same setting may be addressed by the same honorific.

Much of the same behavior is carried on in local French, except that the honorifics *monsieur* (sir), *madame* (ma'am), and *mademoiselle* (miss) are generally substituted for the traditional honorifics derived from kin terms. More recently, the honorifics *citoyen* (male citizen) and *citoyenne* (female citizen) were used by a political-ideological decree from the government in 1971 to distinguish the natives from foreigners.[1] Like the Bantu honorifics based on kin terms, they are generally used alone without the addressees' names. In all such cases, it is generally thought that only deference, not social distance, is expressed. Thus, translations with western European honorifics generally distort the ethnographic meaning somewhat, since they suggest social distance where none is suggested in either the Bantu forms of address with honorifics for deference or the local French adaptations to the system. For instance, the translation of the local French sentence *Suivez-moi, citoyen(ne)* (Follow me, citoyen(ne)) either becomes odd if *citoyen(ne)* is also translated as *citizen* or distorted if it is translated idiomatically as *sir* or *ma'am*. In the latter case, the idiomatic translation assigns higher status to the addressee, whereas the honorific *citoyen(ne)* does not.

Last, aside from the fact that names are generally avoided, it matters little in the Bantu system whether the first name or the surname is used. In any case, to make up for the tradition, speakers of local French often use the traditional Bantu honorifics, the kind of thing that is done less comfortably in a native French setting, unless all the interactants are from the same Bantu background. Note also that, as a rule, French requires that the polite pronoun *vous*, rather than the intimate pronoun *tu*, be used to address people concomitantly with the above titles. In fact, *vous* in the construction *Vous pouvez partir, monsieur/madame* (You may leave, sir/ma'am) assigns high status to the addressee. Using the traditional Bantu honorifics makes allowance for the intimate or status-free pronoun *tu*, which in a construction such as *Tu peux partir, papa* (You may leave, father) conveys both deference and intimacy or lack of status, depending on the case. Using *vous* together with *papa* makes explicit either the higher status of the addressee or the speaker's decision to establish social distance in the interaction.

In my American experience, I had to learn new norms of conduct. Honorifics based on age, and often even on rank, are commonly avoided.[2] My shock started in my first class, when the professor asked to be addressed as Jerry. Most of the other professors did likewise, regardless of age.[3] I found out that generally people do not give their titles when introducing themselves. More often than not, they either give only the first name or ask to be addressed by

---

[1]This custom was patterned on the French system during Napoleon Bonaparte's regime in the nineteenth century to suggest an egalitarian revolution in the way Congolese interact with each other. The corruption and the socioeconomic discriminatory system it was meant to eradicate have grown stronger, starting from the political leadership, and a reactionary trend has now reverted to the current French forms of address with *monsieur* (sir), *madame* (ma'am), or *mademoiselle* (miss) when formality is required.

[2]I will disregard here professional titles such as *Dr.* (for medical doctors) that act as part of the name in professional settings. Constraints are more complex here regarding when the title may be dropped.

[3]There are apparently some exceptions to this observation. In my graduate school experience, I knew of some professors in their sixties that most students addressed as Mr. _____, though their much younger colleagues still addressed them by their first names.

the first name. Further, the first names have usually been clipped to monosyl-labics or disyllabics; for example, *Fred* is short for *Frederick* and *Ed* is short for *Edward*. Sometimes first names have been replaced by seemingly unrelated short nicknames; for example, *Bob* and *Bobby* are short for *Robert* and *Ted* is short for *Edward*. The native French transitional address system according to which persons are addressed by their honorifics and the pronoun *vous*, until there is a tacit or explicit agreement to convert to an intimate and informal mode of address, does not exist in America.

There is more to this American system of address. Foreigners are rebap-tized, so to speak! The often long and "complicated" first names are replaced by nicknames. Ever since my first class, I have usually been addressed as *Sali*. The few Americans that say "Salikoko" either find the name "musical" or want to show off their familiarity with foreign names, in contrast with the regular reaction "I can't say that one."

However, addressing people by their first names does not necessarily mean a close relationship or intimacy. As suggested above, there are ways of express-ing closeness or intimacy, but these will not be discussed here. The American system of address is basically a sign of informality, which is created from the onset of a social relationship, much sooner than I would have expected in the mixed cultural background I came from.

I also learned something else about names. As noted above, it makes lit-tle difference in the Bantu system whether one is addressed by one's first name or by one's surname, whenever names must or can be used. Names are typi-cally avoided when addressing some relations, such as close friends, and names are taboo in addressing or referring to one's own parents. In the case of friends, professional titles or descriptive nicknames dealing with events in one's life are normally used. Name avoidance is a sign of closeness or intimacy. It is con-sidered disrespectful to address ascending and descending in-laws by their names. Their kinship titles must be used not only to express deference but also to reassert the close social bond of the extended family by marriage. The expectation to use kinship honorifics in this case applies even to spouses' rel-atives when they interact among themselves, for instance, when the wife's cousin interacts with the husband's cousin.

The Bantu custom is in sharp contrast with the American custom of using first names or nicknames between close friends and with most in-laws.[4] In the beginning, I found it bizarre to see ascending and descending in-laws (fathers- and mothers-in-law and sons- and daughters-in-law, respectively) address each other by their first names and to see them interact casually with each other. (In my background, ascending and descending in-laws maintain avoidance rela-tionships.) The new custom gave me the impression that Americans did not

---

[4]I do not wish to ignore cases of assimilation where in-laws are addressed by the same kinship titles the spouse uses for them. However, coming from my background, another peculiarity here is that the assimilation applies almost only to the speaker relative to his or her spouse's relatives; his or her own relatives do not assimilate and show intimacy or closeness by using first names.

care much about these special, affined ties and that all social relations were of the same kind. I also assumed then that Americans did not distinguish between acquaintances and friends. In addition, I thought that Americans became personal with people they had just met rather quickly. (This impression was due essentially to the stereotypical French address system I had learned in school.) As noted above, acculturation to American ways has now taken the original shock away. However, coming from my Third World background, there was more to be overwhelmed by than space-age technology.

Acknowledgments

I am grateful to James Armstrong, Kathleen MacQueen, and Jennifer Eason for feedback on drafts of this essay. I alone assume full responsibility for its shortcomings.

15

Arranging a Marriage in India

Serena Nanda

Serena Nanda, who earned her Ph.D. at New York University in 1973, is now a professor at John Jay College of Criminal Justice of the City University of New York. Her field research includes the study of tribal development in India, and her book, Neither Man nor Woman: The Higras of India, *won the 1990 Ruth Benedict Prize. She also has published on ethnicity, gender, and law in the United States, and her interests also include urban and visual anthropology.*

> Sister and doctor brother-in-law invite correspondence from North Indian professionals only, for a beautiful, talented, sophisticated, intelligent sister, 5'3", slim, M.A. in textile design, father a senior civil officer. Would prefer immigrant doctors, between 26–29 years. Reply with full details and returnable photo.

Reprinted from *Stumbling toward Truth: Anthropologists at Work,* edited by Philip R. De Vita (2000), Waveland Press, Inc.

A well-settled uncle invites matrimonial correspondence from slim, fair, educated South Indian girl, for his nephew, 25 years, smart, M.B.A., green card holder, 5'6". Full particulars with returnable photo appreciated.

—Matrimonial Advertisements, *India Abroad*

In India, almost all marriages are arranged. Even among the educated middle classes in modern, urban India, marriage is as much a concern of the families as it is of the individuals. So customary is the practice of arranged marriage that there is a special name for a marriage which is not arranged: It is called a "love match."

On my first field trip to India, I met many young men and women whose parents were in the process of "getting them married." In many cases, the bride and groom would not meet each other before the marriage. At most they might meet for a brief conversation, and this meeting would take place only after their parents had decided that the match was suitable. Parents do not compel their children to marry a person who either marriage partner finds objectionable. But only after one match is refused will another be sought.

As a young American woman in India for the first time, I found this custom of arranged marriage oppressive. How could any intelligent young person agree to such a marriage without great reluctance? It was contrary to everything I believed about the importance of romantic love as the only basis of a happy marriage. It also clashed with my strongly held notions that the choice of such an intimate and permanent relationship could be made only by the individuals involved. Had anyone tried to arrange my marriage, I would have been defiant and rebellious!

At the first opportunity, I began, with more curiosity than tact, to question the young people I met on how they felt about this practice. Sita, one of my young informants, was a college graduate with a degree in political science. She had been waiting for over a year while her parents were arranging a match for her. I found it difficult to accept the docile manner in which this well-educated young woman awaited the outcome of a process that would result in her spending the rest of her life with a man she hardly knew, a virtual stranger, picked out by her parents.

"How can you go along with this?" I asked her, in frustration and distress. "Don't you care who you marry?"

"Of course I care," she answered. "This is why I must let my parents choose a boy for me. My marriage is too important to be arranged by such an inexperienced person as myself. In such matters, it is better to have my parents' guidance."

I had learned that young men and women in India do not date and have very little social life involving members of the opposite sex. Although I could not disagree with Sita's reasoning, I continued to pursue the subject.

"But how can you marry the first man you have ever met? Not only have you missed the fun of meeting a lot of different people, but you have not given yourself the chance to know who is the right man for you."

"Meeting with a lot of different people doesn't sound like any fun at all," Sita answered. "One hears that in America the girls are spending all their time worrying about whether they will meet a man and get married. Here we have the chance to enjoy our life and let our parents do this work and worrying for us."

She had me there. The high anxiety of the competition to "be popular" with the opposite sex certainly was the most prominent feature of life as an American teenager in the late fifties. The endless worrying about the rules that governed our behavior and about our popularity ratings sapped both our self-esteem and our enjoyment of adolescence. I reflected that absence of this competition in India most certainly may have contributed to the self-confidence and natural charm of so many of the young women I met.

And yet, the idea of marrying a perfect stranger, whom one did not know and did not "love," so offended my American ideas of individualism and romanticism, that I persisted with my objections.

"I still can't imagine it," I said. "How can you agree to marry a man you hardly know?"

"But of course he will be known. My parents would never arrange a marriage for me without knowing all about the boy's family background. Naturally we will not rely only on what the family tells us. We will check the particulars out ourselves. No one will want their daughter to marry into a family that is not good. All these things we will know beforehand."

Impatiently, I responded, "Sita, I don't mean know the family, I mean, know the man. How can you marry someone you don't know personally and don't love? How can you think of spending your life with someone you may not even like?"

"If he is a good man, why should I not like him?" she said. "With you people, you know the boy so well before you marry, where will be the fun to get married? There will be no mystery and no romance. Here we have the whole of our married life to get to know and love our husband. This way is better, is it not?"

Her response made further sense, and I began to have second thoughts on the matter. Indeed, during months of meeting many intelligent young Indian people, both male and female, who had the same ideas as Sita, I saw arranged marriages in a different light. I also saw the importance of the family in Indian life and realized that a couple who took their marriage into their own hands was taking a big risk, particularly if their families were irreconcilably opposed to the match. In a country where every important resource in life—a job, a house, a social circle—is gained through family connections, it seemed foolhardy to cut oneself off from a supportive social network and depend solely on one person for happiness and success.

Six years later I returned to India to again do fieldwork, this time among the middle class in Bombay, a modern, sophisticated city. From the experience of my earlier visit, I decided to include a study of arranged marriages in my project. By this time I had met many Indian couples whose marriages had been arranged and who seemed very happy. Particularly in contrast to the fate of many of my married friends in the United States who were already in the process of divorce, the positive aspects of arranged marriages appeared to me to outweigh the negatives. In fact, I thought I might even participate in arranging a marriage myself. I had been fairly successful in the United States in "fixing up" many of my friends, and I was confident that my matchmaking skills could be easily applied to this new situation, once I learned the basic rules. "After all," I thought, "how complicated can it be? People want pretty much the same things in a marriage whether it is in India or America."

An opportunity presented itself almost immediately. A friend from my previous Indian trip was in the process of arranging for the marriage of her eldest son. In India there is a perceived shortage of "good boys," and since my friend's family was eminently respectable and the boy himself personable, well educated, and nice looking, I was sure that by the end of my year's fieldwork, we would have found a match.

The basic rule seems to be that a family's reputation is most important. It is understood that matches would be arranged only within the same caste and general social class, although some crossing of subcastes is permissible if the class positions of the bride's and groom's families are similar. Although dowry is now prohibited by law in India, extensive gift exchanges took place with every marriage. Even when the boy's family do not "make demands," every girl's family nevertheless feels the obligation to give the traditional gifts, to the girl, to the boy, and to the boy's family. Particularly when the couple would be living in the joint family—that is, with the boy's parents and his married brothers and their families, as well as with unmarried siblings—which is still very common even among the urban, upper-middle class in India, the girl's parents are anxious to establish smooth relations between their family and that of the boy. Offering the proper gifts, even when not called "dowry," is often an important factor in influencing the relationship between the bride's and groom's families and perhaps, also, the treatment of the bride in her new home.

In a society where divorce is still a scandal and where, in fact, the divorce rate is exceedingly low, an arranged marriage is the beginning of a lifetime relationship not just between the bride and groom but between their families as well. Thus, while a girl's looks are important, her character is even more so, for she is being judged as a prospective daughter-in-law as much as a prospective bride. Where she would be living in a joint family, as was the case with my friend, the girl's ability to get along harmoniously in a family is perhaps the single most important quality in assessing her suitability.

My friend is a highly esteemed wife, mother, and daughter-in-law. She is religious, soft-spoken, modest, and deferential. She rarely gossips and never quarrels, two qualities highly desirable in a woman. A family that has the reputation for gossip and conflict among its womenfolk will not find it easy to get good wives for their sons. Parents will not want to send their daughter to a house in which there is conflict.

My friend's family were originally from North India. They had lived in Bombay, where her husband owned a business, for forty years. The family had delayed in seeking a match for their eldest son because he had been an Air Force pilot for several years, stationed in such remote places that it had seemed fruitless to try to find a girl who would be willing to accompany him. In their social class, a military career, despite its economic security, has little prestige and is considered a drawback in finding a suitable bride. Many families would not allow their daughters to marry a man in an occupation so potentially dangerous and which requires so much moving around.

The son had recently left the military and joined his father's business. Since he was a college graduate, modern, and well traveled, from such a good family, and, I thought, quite handsome, it seemed to me that he, or rather his family, was in a position to pick and choose. I said as much to my friend.

While she agreed that there were many advantages on their side, she also said, "We must keep in mind that my son is both short and dark; these are drawbacks in finding the right match." While the boy's height had not escaped my notice, "dark" seemed to me inaccurate; I would have called him "wheat" colored perhaps, and in any case, I did not realize that color would be a consideration. I discovered, however, that while a boy's skin color is a less important consideration than a girl's, it is still a factor.

An important source of contacts in trying to arrange her son's marriage was my friend's social club in Bombay. Many of the women had daughters of the right age, and some had already expressed an interest in my friend's son. I was most enthusiastic about the possibilities of one particular family who had five daughters, all of whom were pretty, demure, and well educated. Their mother had told my friend, "You can have your pick for your son, whichever one of my daughters appeals to you most."

I saw a match in sight. "Surely," I said to my friend, "we will find one there. Let's go visit and make our choice." But my friend held back; she did not seem to share my enthusiasm, for reasons I could not then fathom.

When I kept pressing for an explanation of her reluctance, she admitted, "See, Serena, here is the problem. The family has so many daughters, how will they be able to provide nicely for any of them? We are not making any demands, but still, with so many daughters to marry off, one wonders whether she will even be able to make a proper wedding. Since this is our eldest son, it's best if we marry him to a girl who is the only daughter, then the wedding will truly be a gala affair." I argued that surely the quality of the girls themselves made up for any deficiency in the elaborateness of the wedding. My friend admitted this point but still seemed reluctant to proceed.

"Is there something else," I asked her, "some factor I have missed?" "Well," she finally said, "there is one other thing. They have one daughter already married and living in Bombay. The mother is always complaining to me that the girl's in-laws don't let her visit her own family often enough. So it makes me wonder, will she be that kind of mother who always wants her daughter at her own home? This will prevent the girl from adjusting to our house. It is not a good thing." And so, this family of five daughters was dropped as a possibility.

Somewhat disappointed, I nevertheless respected my friend's reasoning and geared up for the next prospect. This was also the daughter of a woman in my friend's social club. There was clear interest in this family and I could see why. The family's reputation was excellent; in fact, they came from a sub-caste slightly higher than my friend's own. The girl, who was an only daughter, was pretty and well educated and had a brother studying in the United States. Yet, after expressing an interest to me in this family, all talk of them suddenly died down and the search began elsewhere.

"What happened to that girl as a prospect?" I asked one day. "You never mention her anymore. She is so pretty and so educated, what did you find wrong?"

"She is too educated. We've decided against it. My husband's father saw the girl on the bus the other day and thought her forward. A girl who 'roams about' the city by herself is not the girl for our family." My disappointment this time was even greater, as I thought the son would have liked the girl very much. But then I thought, my friend is right, a girl who is going to live in a joint family cannot be too independent or she will make life miserable for everyone. I also learned that if the family of the girl has even a slightly higher social status than the family of the boy, the bride may think herself too good for them, and this too will cause problems. Later my friend admitted to me that this had been an important factor in her decision not to pursue the match.

The next candidate was the daughter of a client of my friend's husband. When the client learned that the family was looking for a match for their son, he said, "Look no further, we have a daughter." This man then invited my friends to dinner to see the girl. He had already seen their son at the office and decided that "he liked the boy." We all went together for tea, rather than dinner—it was less of a commitment—and while we were there, the girl's mother showed us around the house. The girl was studying for her exams and was briefly introduced to us.

After we left, I was anxious to hear my friend's opinion. While her husband liked the family very much and was impressed with his client's business accomplishments and reputation, the wife didn't like the girl's looks. "She is short, no doubt, which is an important plus point, but she is also fat and wears glasses." My friend obviously thought she could do better for her son and asked her husband to make his excuses to his client by saying that they had decided to postpone the boy's marriage indefinitely.

By this time almost six months had passed and I was becoming impatient. What I had thought would be an easy matter to arrange was turning out to be quite complicated. I began to believe that between my friend's desire for a girl who was modest enough to fit into her joint family, yet attractive and educated enough to be an acceptable partner for her son, she would not find anyone suitable. My friend laughed at my impatience: "Don't be so much in a hurry," she said. "You Americans want everything done so quickly. You get married quickly and then just as quickly get divorced. Here we take marriage more seriously. We must take all the factors into account. It is not enough for us to learn by our mistakes. This is too serious a business. If a mistake is made we have not only ruined the life of our son or daughter, but we have spoiled the reputation of our family as well. And that will make it much harder for their brothers and sisters to get married. So we must be very careful."

What she said was true and I promised myself to be more patient, though it was not easy. I had really hoped and expected that the match would be made before my year in India was up. But it was not to be. When I left India my friend seemed no further along in finding a suitable match for her son than when I had arrived.

Two years later, I returned to India and still my friend had not found a girl for her son. By this time, he was close to thirty, and I think she was a little worried. Since she knew I had friends all over India, and I was going to be there for a year, she asked me to "help her in this work" and keep an eye out for someone suitable. I was flattered that my judgment was respected, but knowing now how complicated the process was, I had lost my earlier confidence as a matchmaker. Nevertheless, I promised that I would try.

It was almost at the end of my year's stay in India that I met a family with a marriageable daughter whom I felt might be a good possibility for my friend's son. The girl's father was related to a good friend of mine and by coincidence came from the same village as my friend's husband. This new family had a successful business in a medium-sized city in central India and were from the same subcaste as my friend. The daughter was pretty and chic; in fact, she had studied fashion design in college. Her parents would not allow her to go off by herself to any of the major cities in India where she could make a career, but they had compromised with her wish to work by allowing her to run a small dress-making boutique from their home. In spite of her desire to have a career, the daughter was both modest and home-loving and had had a traditional, sheltered upbringing. She had only one other sister, already married, and a brother who was in his father's business.

I mentioned the possibility of a match with my friend's son. The girl's parents were most interested. Although their daughter was not eager to marry just yet, the idea of living in Bombay—a sophisticated, extremely fashion-conscious city where she could continue her education in clothing design—was a great inducement. I gave the girl's father my friend's address and suggested that when they went to Bombay on some business or whatever, they look up the boy's family.

Returning to Bombay on my way to New York, I told my friend of this newly discovered possibility. She seemed to feel there was potential but, in spite of my urging, would not make any moves herself. She rather preferred to wait for the girl's family to call upon them. I hoped something would come of this introduction, though by now I had learned to rein in my optimism.

A year later I received a letter from my friend. The family had indeed come to visit Bombay, and their daughter and my friend's daughter, who were near in age, had become very good friends. During that year, the two girls had frequently visited each other. I thought things looked promising.

Last week I received an invitation to a wedding: My friend's son and the girl were getting married. Since I had found the match, my presence was particularly requested at the wedding. I was thrilled. Success at last! As I prepared to leave for India, I began thinking, "Now, my friend's younger son, who do I know who has a nice girl for him . . . ?"

Further Reflections on Arranged Marriage

The previous essay was written from the point of view of a family seeking a daughter-in-law. Arranged marriage looks somewhat different from the point of view of the bride and her family. Arranged marriage continues to be preferred, even among the more educated, Westernized sections of the Indian population. Many young women from these families still go along, more or less willingly, with the practice, and also with the specific choices of their families. Young women do get excited about the prospects of their marriage, but there is also ambivalence and increasing uncertainty, as the bride contemplates leaving the comfort and familiarity of her own home, where as a "temporary guest" she has often been indulged, to live among strangers. Even in the best situation, she will now come under the close scrutiny of her husband's family. How she dresses, how she behaves, how she gets along with others, where she goes, how she spends her time, her domestic abilities—all of this and much more—will be observed and commented on by a whole new set of relations. Her interaction with her family of birth will be monitored and curtailed considerably. Not only will she leave their home, but with increasing geographic mobility, she may also live very far from them, perhaps even on another continent. Too much expression of her fondness for her own family, or her desire to visit them, may be interpreted as an inability to adjust to her new family, and may become a source of conflict. In an arranged marriage, the burden of adjustment is clearly heavier for a woman than for a man. And that is in the best of situations.

In less happy circumstances, the bride may be a target of resentment and hostility from her husband's family, particularly her mother-in-law or her husband's unmarried sisters, for whom she is now a source of competition for the affection, loyalty, and economic resources of a son or brother. If she is psychologically or even physically abused, her options are limited, as returning to her parents' home or getting a divorce is still very stigmatized. For most Indians, marriage and motherhood are still considered the only suitable roles for a woman, even for those who have careers, and few women can comfortably contemplate remaining unmarried. Most families still consider "marrying off" their daughters as a compelling religious duty and social necessity. This increases a bride's sense of obligation to make the marriage a success, at whatever cost to her own personal happiness.

The vulnerability of a new bride may also be intensified by the issue of dowry that, although illegal, has become a more pressing issue in the consumer conscious society of contemporary urban India. In many cases, where a groom's family is not satisfied with the amount of dowry a bride brings to her marriage, the young bride will be harassed constantly to get her parents to give more. In extreme cases, the bride may even be murdered, and the murder disguised as an accident or a suicide. This also offers the husband's family an opportunity to arrange another match for him, thus bringing in another dowry. This phenomenon, called dowry death, calls attention not just to the "evils of dowry" but also to larger issues of the powerlessness of women as well.

16

Shuar Migrants and Shrunken Heads Face to Face in a New York Museum

Steven L. Rubenstein

Steven Rubenstein is associate professor in the Department of Sociology and Anthropology at Ohio University. He received his PhD from Columbia University in 1995. His research focuses on economic anthropology, colonialism, history, and tourism in the Amazon. He is author of the book Alejandro Tsakimp: A Shuar Healer in the Margins of History.

When I was in the Ecuadorian Amazon in the summer of 1998, the President of the Schuar Federation—a political organization of about 50,000 indigenous

Reprinted from *Anthropology Today*, Vol. 20, no. 3, by permission of Blackwell Publishing, Ltd.

people—showed me twelve *tsantsa,* or shrunken heads, that had recently been de-accessioned from the National Museum of the American Indian. Leaders of the Federation hoped that I could help them develop a plan to build a Schuar museum, in which these heads would be placed along with other items. Thus, when I went to New York in 2003 to visit some Schuar friends, I thought it would be interesting to see what they thought of the shrunken heads on display at the American Museum of Natural History.

Movements of Schuar shrunken heads and Schuar workers are perfect examples of what Arjun Appadurai (1996:33,41) has called an ethnoscope—geography of "moving groups and individuals"—through which culture becomes deterritorialized and globalized. Here I respond to Appadurai's call to study the role of the imagination in the formation of global cultures. However, I take issue with his rejection of models of global culture that rely on a distinction between core and periphery (ibid:31–3). Appadurai argues that global capitalism is too disorganized (that is, lacking a clear and stable center), and that the relationship (and disjunctions) between the economy, culture, and politics is too complex for it to make sense according to the simple binary between core and periphery. However, as I observe it, people everywhere—whether they be in New York or in Ecuador—maintain their own coreperiphery distinction. It is not just that some people identify with the core (or the First World, or civilization) while others identify with the periphery (or the Third World, or savagery), but as I argue here, people who identify themselves in these different ways also imagine the relationship between core and periphery somewhat differently.

Globalization and Culture

A fundamental issue in anthropology is at stake in the core-periphery distinction: how do we talk about non-Western peoples like the Shuar? At the time of contact (and conquest), Europeans were struck by differences, but they also looked for similarities. In the first few centuries following the conquest of the Americas, Europeans debated whether American Indians were living in a state of nature. (If they were living in a state of nature then there was a radical difference between "us," the "civilized," and "they," the "savage." In the nineteenth century most anthropologists came to accept that Indians were similar to us, at least in so far as they too have culture. But some, such as Lewis Henry Morgan, also wondered whether they could go further in their thinking and conceive of an actual connection between them and Westerners. The language of evolution provided a way to express a connection while recognizing (and explaining) differences. In this discourse Indian cultures represented an earlier stage of cultural evolution. (This way of thinking is echoed today in the way people contrast "modern" cultures with "traditional" or "primitive" cultures.) In the twentieth century—especially after World War I—anthropologists largely abandoned this evolutionary model and its implication that Westerners were more advanced than the people they had been conquering and colonizing. Today most people recognize that Indians are not only "cultured," but that their cultures are often quite complex. Although many people still think of them as somehow "more natural" or "closer to nature," anthropologists work rather hard to avoid such language and the implied evolutionary opposition.

For most of the twentieth century, anthropologists were content to study non-Western cultures simply as "different" cultures, and tried to understand them in their own terms. Cultural theorists like Arjun Appadurai are not content to talk only of cultural difference; they have returned to the question of what might connect seemingly different cultures. Most anthropologists had long ago rejected the language of evolution, not just because of ideological doubts about notions of progress, but also because most nineteenth-century evolutionary models were speculative. However, we now have a great many fine historical studies, supplemented by archaeological studies, that help us reconstruct actual changes over the past several hundred years. These studies not only help us understand changes in any particular culture; they show how changes in one culture can lead to (and be influenced by) changes in another. Clearly, cultures need to be understood in terms of larger, even global, contexts.

Anthropologists have long been interested in cultural logics and social structures, so the question now is whether this global context, this world of interacting cultures, itself has a logic, a structure. The terms "core" and "periphery" provide one influential way of talking about a global structure. These terms come from the sociologist Immanuel Wallerstein, who characterized the global market in terms of an unequal division of labour in which low- (or non-) wage-earning workers in "peripheral" countries exchanged goods with high-wage-earning people in "core" countries (Wallerstein 1974:351). The profound insight is that two parts of the world can appear to be radically different (in terms of material wealth, social structure, and values) *precisely because* they have been in a relationship, each influencing each other.

World systems theorists such as Wallerstein were primarily interested in the relationship between different countries (for example Spain and Mexico or England and India). Anthropologists wondered if they could look at relationships between different—even vastly different—cultures in the same way. In his, ironically titled, *Europe and the People without History,* the anthropologist Eric Wolf argued that this core-periphery distinction provides a historical explanation for differences between so-called traditional (or primitive) societies and so-called modern societies, and would thus provide a productive basis for studying local cultures in global terms (Wolf 1982:22–3).

Appadurai (1996:32–43), however, suggests that this distinction functions as a surrogate for the opposition between civilized and savage. He argues that in a world where people and their values (both material and symbolic) circulate so widely and freely, such binary categorizations are anachronistic attempts to impose a false order. Although I share Appadurai's conviction that anthropologists must critique, deconstruct or transcend this opposition, I believe that we must take the distinction between core and periphery seriously—precisely because it helps explain why North Americans and other Westerners have imagined global cultures in terms of a divide between civilized and savage, and also because it helps us understand how and why indigenous people like the Schuar imagine global culture quite differently. This difference has its origin in the nineteenth century, when this ethnoscope first began to emerge.

Discourses of the Collector

In the late nineteenth century Shuar culture was territorialized in the global imagination of Europeans and Euro-Americans through the circulation of shrunken heads. There is evidence that the Shuar and neighbouring groups, collectively called "Jívaro," shrunk the heads of enemies killed in warfare in the 1500s, prior to contact, but there is little evidence that Westerners were interested in this practice until the 1860s. When Euro-Ecuadorians began to settle the region in the 1880s they occasionally traded manufactured goods, like shotguns and machetes, with Shuar, in return for game, salt and shrunken heads. Settlers would sell these heads to dealers in the highlands, who often sold them on to Europeans and North Americans. At the same time the Shuar began to use Western-manufactured shotguns and steel lance-heads in warfare. As Jane Bennet Ross has remarked, the concurrent increase in intergroup warfare and guns-for-heads trade suggests that the Shuar began producing shrunken heads for export (Bennett Ross 1984:89–90; see also Steel 1999:754–9).

It is striking how Euro-Americans despite maintaining their moral and cultural differentiation from the Shuar, actually colluded with the Shuar in trafficking shrunken heads. This paradox is most evident in the story of F. W. Up de Graff and a few other North Americans panning for gold in the upper Amazon in 1899. One day they encountered a large group of Jívaro, who offered them protection from a neighboring group; the prospectors, however, suspected that these Indians were themselves a threat. At first they answered that they could take care of themselves, but then they explained that they themselves were a war-party and invited the Jívaro to join them in attacking a nearby community (Up de Graff 1923:252–3). Although Up de Graff claims that neither he nor his companions fired a shot during the ensuing raid, he does admit to lending his machete to one of the Jívaro, to aid in cutting the head off of a wounded, but still living, woman (1923:274).

Up de Graff admits that readers might misunderstand his motives. He emphasizes that the Jívaro methods of warfare are cowardly and distasteful to the "*true* white man who is brought up to a code of fair play" (1923:270). His heart, he insists, was not really in the butchery; all he really wanted was gold. But this precious metal was not the only thing he wanted to collect. After the slaughter the North Americans chose to stay with their Indian companions, in part, as Up de Graff explains, because "we were anxious to trade the Jívaros out of their trophies" (1923:285). Thus, the mercantile values of the core were crucial to his imagining of the distinction between civilized and savage: the

Jívaro value the heads as trophies of warfare, but for Euro-Americans they are just another precious commodity found in the Amazon.

The Public Closet: Donating That Which Cannot be Discarded

Travelogues like Up de Graff's celebrate the act of collecting discursively. The end results of such acts are celebrated materially in such institutions as the American Museum of Natural History and the National Museum of Natural History. These museums did not acquire most of their shrunken heads through the efforts of adventurous curators or sponsored expeditions.[1] Most were donated by individuals who had come to possess, but did not want, these objects. Robert Carniero, curator of the Hall of South American Indians at the American Museum of Natural History, told me of a widow who had never liked her husband's shrunken head. While he was alive, she insisted that it be kept hidden in a closet; upon his death, she was finally able to get rid of it. On another occasion a young man discovered a head in a warehouse full of his late father's belongings. Informed that the warehouse was to be destroyed, he donated it to the museum. Significantly, none of these people could do what explorers and ethnographers report the Shuar as having done after the shrunken head feast, or after the death of the warrior: throw them away or bury them.[2] Even when unwanted they had to be hoarded and stored in a closet or warehouse. Where even that became unnecessary or impractical then they had to go to a museum—the public's (and public) closet.[3]

The American Museum of Natural History and the Smithsonian Institution, however, are examples of what Mieke Bal called "metamuseums"—large and ambitious museums that display not only their collections, but also older forms of display. In other words, they put themselves, and the very idea of "museums," on display (Bal 1992:260; see also Ames 1986). But they do so in a peculiar way, one that typically highlights the objects of collection while effacing the act of collecting so vividly described in travelogue. Though trophies of colonial expansion acquired by Euro-Ecuadorians in the Upper Amazon, shrunken heads are presented as trophies of Shuar warfare—so museums can present themselves not as collectors of shrunken human heads, but as collectors of tokens of "Shuar culture" (see also Torgovnick 1990 and Feest 1993).

---

[1]Most shrunken heads (though not the ones on actual display) are fakes, testimony to the earlier craze of Euro-Americans to acquire as many shrunken heads as possible.

[2]For a similar clash between non-capitalist and capitalist values, involving the Zuni and the Smithsonian Institution, see Merrill et al., 1993: 546.

[3]Similarly, many of the artefacts owned by museums were originally collected by wealthy private citizens. Those who still wanted to see and show off their stuff, but who had run out of room in their own homes or no longer wanted to pay for the insurance, could donate their private collections to a museum.

These tokens are in turn recontextualized as part of the much larger collection—one that makes sense only to the viewer who has access to the collection as a whole. As Susan Stewart has suggested, such collections privilege the position of the core as the centre of consumption on a global scale (Stewart 1993:162; see also Mitchell 1989).[4] Objects that were originally commodities become something else when they are collected and put on display—used but never used up, they are not so much objects of consumption as fetishes of consumption (Stewart 1993:164).

Although collectors and museum-goers see their distance, and difference, from the Shuar in shrunken heads, ethnographers have suggested that through shrunken heads the Shuar have subordinated difference and distance to social relationships—that is, to terms of affinity rather than alterity. Despite Up de Graff's claims that *tsantsa* were trophies of war, to this day the Shuar are adamant that they are not. Virtually all ethnographers agree that the value of the *tsantsa* lay in its serving as a container for the *muisak*, the avenging spirit of the victim. Some accounts suggest that, through the various rituals of the *tsantsa* feast, the wife of the slayer would have virtual sex with the *muisak*. This act accomplished a "gradual transformation of an unknown foe first into an affine, and at a later stage into a foetus to be born of a woman in the captors' group" (Taylor 1993:671; see Descola 1996a:276). Other accounts suggest that it was the slayer who would dream of, and perform, sexual intercourse with the *muisak*, in order to turn it into his servant (Karsten 1935:367–8). Either way, these rituals express a belief that Carlos Fausto has argued is typical of Amazonia: "the overall reproduction of society is symbolically dependent on relations with the outside and otherness" (Fausto 2000:934).

When Euro-Americans began to offer manufactured instruments of production in return for shrunken heads they transformed this process—for the overall reproduction of Shuar society increasingly came to depend materially on relations with outsiders. In the early years of colonization most Shuar were encouraged by the state to raise cattle and sell lumber, but now Shuar have little to sell to Euro-Americans besides their labour. Leaders of the Federation (see Rubenstein 2001 for a history of the formation of the Federation) are salaried by the state, through agreements with ministries such as health and education, but virtually all Shuar—like their Ecuadorian neighbours—believe they can make more money working in the United States. Though present day Shuar no longer subscribe to the efficacy of *tsantsa* rituals, memories of these rituals nevertheless continue to play an important symbolic role in reproducing Shuar identity. The existence of actual *tsantsa* in North American museums force the Shuar to imagine the global ethnoscope of which they are a part.

---

[4]As Mieke Bal has observed, decontextualization in art collections has a more specific, but comparable, end. Namely, the claim of a universal aesthetic (Bal 1992: 559) and, by implication, the claim of an objective position from which one can recognize this aesthetic.

Finding One's Head

Federation leaders are elected by Shuar, but are financed by the state and foreign NGOs; they represent the Shuar to outsiders, and outsiders to the Shuar. Thus, when the Smithsonian Institution organized the 1991 Festival of American Folklife, they invited Federation officials to consult with curators of the National Museum of the American Indian who were selecting objects for exhibition. At the request of these leaders, the museum returned twelve *tsantsa* to the Shuar Federation on 6 October 1995. For well over a century, it was only from the point of view of Euro-Americans (especially given the way *tsantsa* were displayed in museums) that the heads represented "the Shuar"; it was in part because of this metonymic function that the National Museum of the American Indian repatriated the heads to the Shuar Federation—they recognized the Federation as the legitimate representative of the Shuar (and, at the time, Achuar) people.[5] The return of the heads accomplished more than a recognition of the legitimacy of the Shuar Federation; the Federation claims to represent the Shuar nation and in this sense it could be construed as the restoration of a new political body (see Winans 1994 for a similar case in East Africa).

My Shuar friends in New York, however, expressed no interest in the repatriation of the heads at the American Museum of Natural History. Overwhelmed by the size of the museum, they immediately grasped its function to represent the power of the core. This power was communicated to them most immediately, although ambiguously, as we climbed the steps to the main entrance and they saw people lining up to present themselves to guards. They panicked, because they had no identification with them and spoke only Spanish—they were afraid of being detained. I explained that in fact the authorities of the museum were afraid of a terrorist attack, and that the guards were merely checking people's bags. As we silently submitted to the cursory search I realized how a form of power I took for granted appeared to my friends as unpredictable and was easily misunderstood.

The museum also confirmed their sense that New York is at the centre of the world, while their awareness of their inability to read signs in English reminded them of their own peripheral status. At the same time, they experienced their position as consumers of the collection as liberating and exciting. When I later asked them what their favorite parts of the museum had been they did not mention the *tsantsa*, but rather what was exotica for them: the stuffed animals from Africa, gemstones and asteroids. They also emphasized that they saw only a small portion of the collections, and saw in their visit an opportunity to belong to a much bigger world than that they had previously imagined.

---

[5]What occurred was not technically repatriation, as the National Museum of the American Indian had no legal obligation to give the heads to the Shuar Federation. They were given out of a sense of ethical obligation.

For similar reasons, they were content for the heads to remain in the museum: they still see *tsantsa* as a way to experience others in terms of relationships, rather than absolute difference. They assumed that just as they were interested in learning more about North American culture, the presence of the heads in the museum expressed North American interest in Shuar culture; moreover, they felt that the heads represent a Shuar presence in the centre of the world. Yet they commented on the fact that the heads were presented out of context—not just cultural, but also historical context. It is, I believe, this lack of historical context rather than the actual physical location of the heads that signals the peripheral status of the Shuar. To the Shuar this lack of context was tantamount to a lack of a sort of recognition, for they internalize the heads in terms of a complex sort of otherness. They do not see the heads as representing who they are (because they themselves do not shrink heads); the heads represent who they are *not*. In the nineteenth century what was important was that the heads were not Shaur, but were rather taken from the neighbouring Achuar (with whom they sometimes traded). Today this difference is no longer important; what matters is that the heads were not taken and shrunk by them, but by their ancestors. Either way, this "not" is never an absolute negativity. In the past it expressed not only distance but also proximity; today it expresses not only distance but also possession. They identify the heads with *their* ancestors. Thus the heads now serve as markers of their own past—in short, the heads are the most material and visible means they have for identifying themselves as a people with history.

The distance between the Shuar and their past—between these migrant workers in New York and their head-shrinking grandfathers or great-grandfathers—constitutes a largely unknown territory. Until recently the Shuar lacked a written history; even today the written history available to them is superficial and simplistic, and largely takes the form of textbooks for children. Moreover, since such textbooks have mostly been written by missionaries or government bureaucrats, they reflect the ideological interests of the Church or the State.

Some books written by missionaries who have adopted an ethnographic voice, or even by Western ethnographers and translated into Spanish, do attempt to provide an "authentic" portrait of the Shuar. Yet Shuar are often confused or even alienated by these books, which describe, in the present tense, a way of life that is foreign to them. Of course they understand that these books were written many decades ago, and are meant to represent the past—but the stories these books tell do not even correlate with the stories their parents or grandparents used to tell. I do not think this means that classic ethnographies of the Shuar are wrong or mistaken. It might simply be that the story a Shuar would tell an anthropologist and the story a Shuar would tell his grandchild would be different: both stories equally partial, both stories equally true—but in different ways.

But I do know that the books the Shuar read about their own culture represent a dated, and in some ways, dubious project. For example, when

Michael Harner wrote his classic ethnography *Jívaro: People of the Sacred Waterfalls* he worked within the twentieth-century paradigm of describing a culture in its own terms. Harner was delighted when, in the 1978 Spanish translation of his book, Aíjiu Juank wrote a preface explaining how the ethnography had value for Shuar, as it would "help us to rediscover our dignity and to regain the equilibrium that we need for an authentic development, based on our own values" (quoted in Harner 1984:xv). Harner did not know that Aíjiu Juank was actually Alfredo Germani, an Italian born Catholic missionary—which raises the question of whether this ethnography was being used to promote Shuar values or missionary values. This is a practical and a political question for many Shuar, who have concluded that missionary attempts to isolate Shuar from Ecuadorian society (in the course of what Germani calls "authentic development"), far from protecting them, only made Shuar dependent on missionaries for access to the larger world.

Today, Federation officials no longer depend on missionaries, and travel not only to Quito (the capital of Ecuador) but also to Europe and the United States (in order to participate in international conferences). Other Shuar, like my friends, travel to Los Angeles or New York in search of jobs. When they come upon *tsantsa* in a New York museum they not only encounter a physical piece of their past, but also evidence that their grandparents and great-grandparents also participated in a world system. The Shuar claim this territory as their own not in the sense that it is exclusively theirs—like their grandparents, whether in Ecuador or New York they share space with others—but in the sense that an understanding of others might explain who they are and how they came to be. They are not sure what such an explanation might actually be, and as we stood by the display they shared some of the stories their fathers or grandfathers had told them. Ultimately, I believe, their curiosity about this moving past, this ethnoscope, is closely bound up with their own claim to territory.

Imagining History

As we spent over an hour lingering by the heads, and watching people pass by without so much as glancing at them, they began to suspect that their own imagining of this ethnoscope was different from that of others. I had hoped for (or rather, tried to contrive) encounters between my friends and other visitors, but I had forgotten how strong the invisible walls between people are when so many crowd together in one place. Of the dozens of people who passed the shrunken heads, only a few paused to look at them. One of my friends, who knows a few words of English, introduced himself, and I explained who we were. "They are beautiful, yes?" my friend asked. The others visitors looked startled, but said "yes." My friend spoke in Spanish and I translated: "He says that his grandparents made these, although Shuar no longer hunt heads." The other visitor said, "Yes, we know." We stood together for a few more moments, without saying anything, and the other visitor walked away.

My Shuar friends found the apparent passivity of visitors striking. They saw me as a local guide, translating and explaining different exhibits for them, and thought that the South American Hall should provide visitors with Indian guides who, they felt, would not only provide better explanations of Amazonian past: their very presence would reveal the Amazonian present—and the evident contrast between the present and past would demonstrate that Indians like the Shuar are peoples with history. They were sure this would be of profound interest to most visitors.

Others have argued that historical knowledge is partial and culturally mediated. I suggest here that people from the core and from the periphery mediate it in radically different ways—that is, we have very different attitudes towards our amnesias. In this the Shuar are strikingly different form other museum goers, who see "natural history," a history of the ontological other, and have forgotten the sociological history, the history of the political-economy by which these objects came to reside in one building in New York. Thus, whenever I ask my students who have seen shrunken heads what they thought, they ask me, "How did Shuar make them?" But when we returned to the apartment of one of my Shuar friends and, over dinner, I asked them what they thought of the museum exhibit, they all wanted to know, "How did our *tsantsa* end up in New York?" We all forget parts of our past, but some of us want to remember more than others.

References

Ames, Michael M. 1986. *Museums, the public and anthropology: A study in the anthropology of anthropology.* Vancouver: Ranchi Anthropology Series 9.

Appadurai, Arjun 1996. *Modernity at large: Cultural dimensions of globalization.* Minneapolis: University of Minnesota Press.

Bal, Mieke 1992. Telling, showing, showing off. *Critical Inquiry* 18(3): 556–594.

Bennett Ross, Jane 1984. Effects of contact on revenge hostilities among the Achuara Jívaro. In Ferguson, R.B. (ed.) *Warfare, culture, and environment* pp 83–124. Orlando: Academic Press.

Descola, P. 1996a. *The spears of twilight,* trans. Janet Lloyd. New York: The New Press.

Fausto, C. 2000. Of enemies and pets: Warfare and shamanism in Amazonia. *American Ethnologist* 26(4): 933–56.

Feest, C.F. 1993. Comments on "The return of the *Ahayu:da.*" *Current Anthropology* 34(5): 83–124.

Harner, M. 1984. *Jívaro: People of the sacred waterfalls.* Berkeley: University of California Press.

Karsten, R. 1935. *The headhunters of Western Amazonas. The life and culture of the Jíbaro Indians of eastern Equador and Peru.* Helsinki: Societas Scientiarum Fennica, Commentationes Humanarum Littararum VII(I).

Merrill, W.L., Ladd, E.J. and Ferguson, T.J. 1993. "The return of the *Ahayu:da.*" *Current Anthropology* 34(5), pp 83–124.

Mitchell, T. 1989. The world as exhibition. *Comparative Studies in Society and History* 31(1): 217–236.

Morgan, L.H. 1978. [1877] *Ancient Society* New York: Holt and Company.

Rubenstein, S. 2001. Colonialism, the Shuar Federation, and the Ecuadorian state. *Environment and Planning D: Society and Space* 19(3): 263–93.

Steel, D. 1999. Trade goods and Jívaro warfare: The Shuar 1850–1957, and the Achuar, 1940–1978. *Ethnohistory* 46(4): 745–76.

Stewart, S. 1993. *On longing: Narratives of the miniature, the gigantic, the souvenir, the collection.* Durham: Duke University Press.

Taylor, A.-C. 1993. Remembering to forget: Identity, mourning and memory among the Jívaro. *Man* 28(4): 653–678.

Torgovnick, M. 1990. *Gone primitive.* Chicago: The University of Chicago Press.

Up de Graff, F.W. 1923. *Head hunters of the Amazon: Seven years of exploration and adventure.* Garden City: Garden City Publishing Company, Inc.

Wallerstein, I. 1974. *The modern world system.* New York: Academic Press.

Winans, E.V. 1994. The head of the king: Museums and the path to resistance. *Comparative Studies in Society and History* 36(2): 221–241.

Wolf, E. 1982. *Europe and the people without history.* Berkeley: The University of California Press.